SIX SECONDS
TO **GLORY**

It's not just a six-second run, you know. It seems like six hours building up to run six seconds. It starts back in the pits and works its way to where you pull in beside the guy you are going to race. And he looks at you. And you look at him. Six seconds sometimes feels like a lifetime—especially when you look out the side and there's a car right next to you.
                    —Don Prudhomme

SIX SECONDS
TO GLORY

DON "THE SNAKE" PRUDHOMME'S
HAIR-RAISING 1973 FUNNY CAR RACE

HAL HIGDON

OCTANE
PRESS
octanepress.com

Originally published by Putnam (1975)
under ISBN 978-0399204470

Octane Press, Edition 2.1, October 29, 2013
Copyright © 2013 by Octane Press

ISBN 978-1-937747-27-5

Typeset by Carol Weiss
Copyedited by Leah Noel
Cover and Interior Design by Tom Heffron

ON THE COVER: Images of Don Prudhomme. *Steve Reyes*

Printed in the United States

octanepress.com

Contents

Introduction

I first met Don Prudhomme, the Snake, while writing *Finding the Groove*, a book on the sport of auto racing that was published in 1973. The book featured interviews with twenty-seven leading drivers of the era: everyone from Richard Petty to Mario Andretti to Mark Donahue.

Three were drag racers: Don Garlits, then the number one driver in the top fuel division; Don Prudhomme, who was equally dominant in funny cars; and Malcolm Garrett, a street racer from my hometown of Michigan City, Indiana. Malcolm never achieved the level of drag racing fame as Garlits or Prudhomme, but years later, Malcolm switched sports, serving as corner man for heavyweight champion Mike Tyson.

In each chapter of *Finding the Groove*, I asked the driver: "How do you go fast around a racetrack?" The book featured their answers. Some drivers understood their sport better than others, or at least had the ability to communicate their understanding better.

My interview with Snake was brief and workmanlike. His chapter occupied a relatively modest four pages, compared to the sixteen-page chapter that featured Indy 500 champion and certified wildman Bobby Unser. The best I can say about my first meeting with Don Prudhomme was that he was polite.

Snake and I met at his garage in Van Nuys, California. We drove in my rental car to a nearby drive-in for lunch. He ordered a hamburger and a Coke. I mentioned that I was heading to Phoenix to meet a tire-testing Bobby Unser next. Interestingly, Snake spent as much time asking me about other drivers interviewed for *Finding the Groove* as I spent quizzing him. While many drivers focused intently on their own branch of auto racing, not wasting much energy on other branches, Snake showed a willingness to learn from everyone. He even had picked up some tips from Indy champion A. J. Foyt: "He told us we were out to lunch with the angle we were running our wings."

"Was he right?" I asked.

"Yeah, he was," admitted Don Prudhomme, who also confessed to caging tips from NASCAR teams.

Most interesting, Snake talked about the importance of the machine vs. the man driving the machine: "You need the car set up right," Snake said while finishing his hamburger. "The rest is getting into it and leaving at the right time and steering going down the course. But it's not so much that one driver is better than another driver. It's more the machinery and the mechanical end to it. The car plays a big part in whether you're going to win or lose the race."

Don Prudhomme took one final sip of his Coke, then we climbed back into my rental car, and I drove him back to his garage, with me flying later that day to meet Bobby Unser in Phoenix.

Two years passed before I saw Snake again. I then had a contract to write a book about drag racing, not necessarily about any single individual, but about the sport. My editor at G. P. Putnam told me to go to the drag nationals in Indianapolis and, "write about what you see."

So I hung out in the pits for a couple of days and watched the eliminations that eventually would pit the two top drivers in each category in final run-offs against each other. Funny cars then took six seconds to run a quarter mile, so that eventually became my book title: *Six Seconds to Glory*.

At some point during the weekend, I reintroduced myself to Snake, who may or may not have remembered our lunch in Van Nuys. I knew he was preoccupied working on his car between heats, so I did not seek an immediate interview. Only after his semifinal win over Leroy Goldstein, which qualified him for the finals against Ed McCulloch, did I move to his pits to watch Snake prepare his car for the final run. Rather than take notes, I used a camera to record what I saw, shooting several hundred photos.

After the winners in all categories had been crowned, I drove to my home in Northern Indiana and had the photos developed, creating a scrapbook chronicling the actions of Snake and his crew between the semifinals and finals. Then I called Don Prudhomme and told him, "I have something I want to show you." Ever polite, when you caught him away from the competitive milieu, Snake invited me to visit him at his home.

After arriving, I set the scrapbook on a table and opened it to the first page, featuring a picture of Snake climbing out of his car after his semifinal win. "What were you thinking about when I took that picture?" I asked. And continued to ask that question about each picture in the scrapbook.

Snake got it instantly. He enthusiastically bought into the project. The result was a series of responses that opened a door into the mind of the man who at that point in time was the most successful funny car driver on the planet.

And thus this book, among my best, one I am proud to see in print again.

     — Hal Higdon
       Long Beach, Indiana
       Spring 2013

1

"I'M IN TROUBLE"

Don Prudhomme flashed toward the finish line at more than 200 mph, the engine of his Cuda race car screaming, the car itself a yellow blur. He reached for the parachute release over his head and yanked, at the same time lifting his foot from the throttle. *Woomph!* A blue canopy popped open behind him as he crossed the line. The car began to slow, its engine now silent. Prudhomme allowed the Cuda, its chute rotating gently in the breeze, to roll on down the track past the exit where most drivers turn off before he pulled the hand brake.

Prudhomme, who lived in Granada Hills, California, was the only driver among 1,300 entrants at the Nationals who used the entire length of the drag strip to stop. He did this for several reasons. First, the regular exit was fairly close to the finish line and featured a sharp 180-degree turn; he didn't want to strain his car by braking hard and turning quickly. Secondly, Don

Prudhomme (perhaps best known by his nickname Snake) prefers doing things his own way. But mostly, he wanted time alone at the end of the runway to think about his last run and the one to come.

As Don Prudhomme rolled to a halt, he was thinking: *I'm in trouble.*

He thought he was in trouble despite his having defeated Leroy Goldstein to qualify for the finals in the funny car class at the most important drag championship of the year, the U.S. Nationals, held each Labor Day weekend at Indianapolis Raceway Park. At that moment Goldstein was back at the other turnoff, climbing out the side window of his car so he could fold his collapsed chute and go home.

Leroy Goldstein had come off the starting line the same instant as Don Prudhomme. "It was a dead even start," Leroy would remember. The cars had roared off down the black, two-lane, asphalt pavement, fender to fender. The heads of 60,000 spectators turned to follow the action. At 150 feet off the line, Goldstein seemed to have a very slender lead. Had he time to express his feelings, however, Prudhomme would have exhibited no worry. He had set his car up to run best at top speed. "There's a place at mid-track where it normally makes its good move." Snake would explain later. "That's where it comes on hard."

But at 150 feet clouds of smoke began to rise behind Snake's car. His clutch had locked on him, transmitting too much power to the wheels and causing the tires to spin on the racetrack, in effect "smoking" them as the rubber burned. Although a drag racing car may look as if it's going faster with smoke pouring from behind, actually it's going slower because of lost traction. Goldstein should have pulled away at this point, except for the fact that he also was smoking his tires.

Halfway down the track the smoke vanished from behind both cars as their tires once more bit into the track. Prudhomme made that "good move" he talked about and pulled ahead to a full car-length advantage as he reached the first timing light, sixty-six feet from the finish line. But only the width of a wheel separated him from defeat at the actual finish line.

Prudhomme, whose temper flares easily, later bristled at comments that he almost had lost the race by popping his chute too soon. "It's not exactly the first time I've driven that car on a racetrack," he snapped. "I knew where I was." He wasn't interested in looking behind. He was looking ahead. He knew he had qualified for the finals and a shot at a first-place prize, which would come to $15,000.

Drag racing is probably the simplest of all motor sports. A drag race consists of two cars that move to the starting line, wait until a green light flashes before them, and then race fender to fender down a long, straight track. No turns are involved, as in a race like the Indianapolis 500. The first one to complete a quarter mile is the winner. So swift are the funny cars that race at drag strips that they cover this quarter mile in roughly six seconds, reaching speeds around 230 mph.

If one of the drivers should cross the starting line before the green light, a red light flashes showing he is disqualified. He also may be disqualified should he cross the center line dividing the two-lane track. Once a driver wins his race, he usually returns quickly to the pits to prepare his car for the next round.

At the Nationals more than 1,300 drivers were competing in 121 classes for $351,000 in prizes. The three top professional classes are: dragster, pro stock, and funny car. It is the funny car class that most excites the fans. Seventy-one funny car drivers had entered the field when the Nationals began on Wednesday with technical inspection and practice. By Sunday evening this field had been reduced to the sixteen fastest qualifiers, with Don Prudhomme at the top of the list.

These sixteen faced off in eight two-man races early Monday afternoon. The eight survivors raced again an hour later—and then there were four. Those four met in the two semifinal heats. Prudhomme, having won his heat, would meet the winner of the second heat in the finals. At that moment it was 3:55 P.M. He would have nearly an hour and a half to solve the clutch problems that had caused him to smoke his tires.

But he had another problem. He also worried that he might have "hurt" his engine. A racing engine must be finely tuned, like a violin. A violinist can tell when his violin is out of tune, and so can a skilled driver tell the tune of his engine. Snake had noticed a roughness in his engine's sound as he crossed the finish line, as though one of its eight cylinders was misfiring. He thought maybe he had burned a piston, although he would have to wait until he returned to the pits to find out.

Prudhomme unsnapped his shoulder harness. He pulled off his fireproof gloves, unfastened his goggles, and removed his crash helmet. He set the helmet upside down on the metal support in front of the Cuda's steering wheel, placing gloves and goggles inside it. He next tugged loose his gas mask and hood, items designed to permit him survival in a fire. He swore loudly.

Prudhomme gritted his teeth. His hair was matted and damp. His brow was furrowed and covered with sweat. He made no attempt to wipe his brow with the forearm of his fire suit because the suit was covered with a layer of oil, rubber, and dirt, the residue from hundreds of runs down a drag strip. The shut-off engine crackled as it cooled. Snake leaned forward, shoulders bent, slumped over the steering wheel. A drop of sweat rolled off the end of his nose. He swore again.

The sun beat down on the Cuda's yellow roof. It was a hot, muggy, uncomfortable day with the temperature ninety-one degrees and the humidity 50 percent. Only a southwest wind provided occasional relief. Yet Snake remained seated in his racer and continued to worry about the finals of the funny car field.

Last year at this same time he had also appeared at the Nationals. He then was driving a fuel dragster, actually the fastest drag-racing class. Fuel dragsters are sometimes called rails because of their slender, rail-like bodies. A funny car actually is a shortened dragster with a fiberglass body that makes the machine look somewhat like a street car. Prudhomme in 1973 was trying for his first national championship in a funny car, having won at Indy in 1965,

1969, and 1970 in a dragster. No other driver ever had won four victories at the Nationals. Only one other driver (Don Garlits, also with three wins) had ever come close.

In 1972 Prudhomme had failed to win that fourth victory because he had smoked his tires at the starting line in a quarter-final run. To make a car go fast, you must achieve a delicate balance that includes a powerful engine, properly adjusted clutch, sticky tires, and a dry track. Prudhomme had come close and had failed in 1972, and he faced failure again unless he could obtain the proper balance. He had been lucky to beat Goldstein, and he knew it. He couldn't rely on luck to carry him through the next round. "You just can't go back, make another run, and hope it won't smoke the tires again," he was to say. "You've got to change. You've got to readjust the combination."

The truck carrying Prudhomme's crew approached, a cloud of dust rising behind. The crew hurried to reach their driver, so they could get the race car back to the pits to be worked on for the next round. The cast of helpers, which had swollen to nearly a dozen at Indianapolis, included Don Prudhomme's two regular crewmen, Bob Brandt and Jerry Herrier.

Bob Brandt, a small mustached young man who answered to the nickname Weasel, had worked three years with Snake and served as chief mechanic. Stockily built Jerry Herrier had joined the team in March. Previously he had worked for Tony Nancy and Dwight Salsbury.

As the truck skidded to a halt beside the race car, Weasel leaned out the driver's window and shouted, "You ran a fifty-two." He referred to the 6.52 seconds it had taken Prudhomme to cover the quarter mile, not a very good time considering he had qualified yesterday in 6.35 and run 6.27 in his first heat.

"Come on, get moving!" Prudhomme shouted. His voice echoed hollowly, but loudly, from inside the race car.

"Whew, Snake's hot," Jerry mumbled. He jumped from the truck and ran over to the hood of the race car. Pulling the catch holding the Cuda's fiberglass body in place, Jerry tilted the body upward. Weasel slipped a pair of poles under the nose to hold it up. The flip-top body is one reason for the name funny car.

Prudhomme climbed out of his seat still swearing and shouting at nobody in particular. He stalked over to the truck and threw his helmet into the back seat. He almost tore his fire jacket off and dumped it on top of the helmet. Underneath he wore a wild, decorative white T-shirt with the name of several sponsors across the front—Wynn's, Cragar, Bell Helmets, Hot Wheels—and the picture of a cobra poised to strike.

Don Prudhomme resembles the picture of a snake on his chest. He is tall, lean, hipless. He stands six feet one inch and weighs 160 pounds. He has broad but humped shoulders not unlike a hooded cobra. A snake strikes swiftly; so does Don Prudhomme at the wheel of his car.

He also has dark, curly hair and flashing eyes. His chin is long, his jaw sharp. The name Prudhomme in French means "proud man." It is an apt label, but he is perhaps best known by his nickname. A lot of people don't know the man Don Prudhomme, but they've heard of the Snake.

At that moment a loud rumble echoed from the starting line nearly three-quarters of a mile away. Ed McCulloch had just done a burnout, shooting across the line to warm his tires. He was racing Sush Matsubara in the other semifinal round. A few seconds passed, and there came another rumble from Matsubara. Large clouds of smoke covered the starting area. Both drivers backed up following their burnouts, their engines popping.

Don Prudhomme moved back toward his race car. "You smoked the tires," Weasel told him.

"Yeah."

"How did the engine run?"

"Problems."

There was a sudden hiss from under the car. Jerry had tripped the valve releasing steam from the engine. Funny cars, unlike regular automobiles, do not have radiators. They run for only a few minutes at a time, thus do not need radiators for cooling purposes. To a certain extent the more heat in a fuel engine, the more power it produces. Water is used in the cylinder blocks mainly to equalize pressure and prevent the engine from seizing.

Weasel picked the parachute up off the ground and tossed it onto the Cuda's rear deck. Another larger rumble sounded from the direction of the starting line. McCulloch and Matsubara were racing. The rumble increased in pitch as the two cars approached. By the time the sound of their engines reached Snake's ears, McCulloch and Matsubara were nearly at half track, and by the time the sound stopped the two drivers were drifting, parachutes open, toward the turnoff.

Prudhomme, wiping his forehead with a towel, glanced down the track in time to see one of the lane lights signal a victory. It did not register in his mind at the moment which driver, McCulloch or Matsubara, had won.

The winner of the other semifinal heat, in fact, was Ed McCulloch of Fresno, California. McCulloch had won the funny car title at the Nationals the previous two years. Having qualified again for the finals, he now had a chance to make it three in a row. Only Don Prudhomme stood in his way.

"It was a pretty close race with Sush," McCulloch would later explain. "In my earlier heats I never saw the other car. Now either he made a better move or I was late. He left the starting line, and I could see him. My car picked the front end up and went out. I set the front end down and put him away. The car didn't seem to want to run through the middle, but that's where I pulled him."

McCulloch had an e.t. (elapsed time) of 6.48 seconds against 6.55 for Matsubara. In the previous heat, Prudhomme had run 6.52. The e.t. is measured from the moment the car leaves the starting line, breaking the photoelectric light beam wired to the clocks. When the car crosses the finish line a quarter mile further down the track, it trips another light beam, stopping the clocks, which are capable of measuring time to a thousandth of a second.

The speed in miles per hour at the finish also is computed through the use of two additional sets of light beams, one 66 feet before the finish line and the other 66 feet beyond it. The National Hot Rod Association, which sponsors the U.S. Nationals, maintains records in both elapsed time and miles per hour. Ironically, despite his many victories at NHRA meets, big and small, Don Prudhomme never had held an official NHRA quarter-mile record in either e.t. or mph.

"Records are a kind of ego thing." Snake says. "They don't really mean much. It's nice when you have them, but I wouldn't go out of my way to get one. I wouldn't put my car through the pains and strains of trying to get a record and possibly sacrifice a motor. I don't need that." Victory, however, is something else. Prudhomme later admitted that if it had been necessary to burn his $20,000 race car to the ground in order to win at the Nationals, he would have done just that.

Don Prudhomme handed the towel to Weasel. Despite the heat, he had not removed his boots and bulky fire trousers, which had "Snake" lettered in the sides. He didn't want to take time to change.

"We're going to have to get on that clutch," he told his crew.

"You also have an oil leak," said Weasel, pointing to a black puddle forming beneath the car.

Snake grunted and climbed back into the Cuda's seat. Jerry lowered the body around him as Weasel threw the support rods in the back of the truck. Most funny car drivers return to the pits with bodies propped open. Don Prudhomme, who usually operates differently from everybody else, returns to the pits top down. He must endure more heat, but his crew can return faster since there will be no danger of a sudden bump knocking the top down.

The crowd has a hard time seeing the driver either way. The driver sits in what would be the back seat of a normal car. The rear half of the engine occupies the front seat space. The driver must peer down the track through a windshield that is little more than a narrow slit. The supercharger atop the engine sticks up through the windshield, further blocking the forward view. There are no doors, only open side windows, through which the driver may have to tumble in a hurry in case of fire. The driver never wants to see anything outside that side window during a race. If he sees the other car, it probably means he is losing.

While being towed along the return road past the regular turnoff, Prudhomme at last discovered the identity of the other finalist. The crewmen buzzing around Ed McCulloch had smiles on their faces. Sush Matsubara's crew were still driving, moving up the road, in no hurry to face their driver.

Even though he knew the answer, Snake shouted to McCulloch as he passed: "Did you win?"

McCulloch, a stocky man with rumpled brown hair, simply nodded his head.

It was down now to two men: one six-second run for the money. The previous day when Ed McCulloch obtained a copy of the pairings, he had sat down to predict the winners in each of the four rounds. He was playing guessing games, but for a purpose. He wanted to know whom he would have to beat to defend his title. In handicapping the field this way, he correctly predicted every race to that point, including that he would meet Don

Prudhomme in the finals. When Snake had arrived at the track early that morning, he saw McCulloch and asked, "What round will we run?"

"The last round," said McCulloch.

"Great," said Snake, and the two men smiled grimly at each other, like two gunslingers who had just made a date to meet on Main Street at high noon. Though neither said another word, both were thinking that was the way it should be. Fate should decree that the two champions meet in the finals rather than in some lesser round. Then each man had gone about the business of preparing his car.

Now they had come almost to that last round. In another hour and a half they would meet. Victory would be decided in six swift seconds. Yet the drama had only begun.

Weasel slowed the truck as they approached a building near the finish line. Ed Kissinger, an NHRA official, offered him a small slip of paper. "Give it to the driver," Weasel instructed. Kissinger bent and handed the slip to Snake as his Cuda was towed past. Snake glanced at the slip of paper, which recorded the time and speed of his last run. He frowned and thrust the slip deep into the pocket of his fire suit as though he didn't want to see it again.

As Snake's car passed the grandstand, the people applauded his semifinal victory. Some cheered. Some waved. The crewmen in the truck responded by waving back and grinning and flashing victory signs, but Don Prudhomme himself was in another world. He was completely unaware of the crowd's applause. He would think about it later and remember it was there, but at that moment he was staring dourly at his steering wheel.

When he had smoked his tires on the previous round, the rear end had risen as the tires expanded from the heat. The balance of the 2,200-pound race car had shifted from rear to front wheels. The car had begun to drift sideways. Prudhomme had had to grapple with the steering wheel to keep pointed straight down the track. Now, as he stared at the steering wheel, he noticed it was cocked to one side, indicating that something was broken or at least out of line.

More trouble, he thought. It was another item that would have to be fixed before he could meet Ed Mc-Culloch in the final round.

2

"I ALWAYS LIKED CARS"

Don Prudhomme, in reaching the finals of the Nationals, had come a long way from where he had grown up, a car-crazy kid in the San Fernando Valley of Southern California. Don's father had come from Texas, his mother from Louisiana. They met and moved to Los Angeles, where Don was born on April 6, 1941. He had an older brother, named Monette, and he later had three younger sisters: Judy, Joyce, and Jeanette.

Not long after Don's birth the Prudhomme family moved over the first range of hills north of the Los Angeles city limits into the San Fernando Valley. The communities in the Valley include Burbank, North Hollywood, Van Nuys, and Granada Hills. To a person from out-of-state it all seems a part of the Los Angeles urban sprawl, but those who grew up there consider themselves residents of the Valley, not L.A.

"I always liked cars," Snake remembers. "My dad had this body shop. Even as a little kid I would help him. You know: hold the bumper, tighten a bolt, or something like that. He'd lend his customers old junk Dodges while he worked on their automobiles. So I used these cars to stick around in. I learned to drive while pretty young. My dad used to put me between his legs and let me hold the steering wheel while he was driving down the road. By the time I got my driver's license I was a whiz. Passed with flying colors."

Don Prudhomme's life story can almost be retold by relating what he has driven. Thus: Mustang Motorcycle, '48 Merc, '50 Olds, '55 Buick, 27-T roadster, AA fuel dragster, funny car. At fourteen Don delivered newspapers, earning enough to buy the motorcycle, what would be called a minibike today. He hadn't owned it long before he forgot to lock the garage door one night and it was stolen. He and Tom McCourry, a close friend, next obtained jobs with a gardener who drove a vintage LaSalle with lawn mowers, rakes, and baskets tied to the bumpers and running boards. "It was a grim-looking unit," Snake recalls. "We wanted to be cool and couldn't be seen by our friends riding in it." So he and McCourry would slump down in the back seat when the LaSalle rumbled past one of their downtown Van Nuys hangouts. Prudhomme recalls placing a box over his head one time to avoid being seen by a friend.

He bought a '48 Mercury with the earnings from his next job: collecting eggs and feeding chickens at a nearby ranch. Unfortunately he had only a learner's permit, and his mother had to accompany him when he drove it. He soon traded up to a '50 Oldsmobile. He and McCourry would spend their weekends at the drags, either San Fernando Drag Strip or Saugus Drag Strip.

The year was 1957, and organized drag racing was barely a decade old. People had started using Southern California's dry lake beds for straightaway races in the thirties. They measured off quarter-mile courses on airport runways in the forties. Kids meanwhile would street-race on back roads. As the sport grew in popularity, promoters built tracks specially for drag racing. Saugus was one of those early tracks.

The number one hero at Saugus in the mid-fifties was Dick Harriman, who drove a '49 Oldsmobile, minus a front bumper, with wedges jammed in the springs to make the nose stick up and painted from the windshield forward with a dull-gray primer coat. "It looked kind of cool," Snake remembers. "At least I thought it looked neat. Of course, if a guy didn't have any roof, I thought it looked cool. Harriman would just kill everybody at the drags, so I copied how his car looked, primered the front end, the whole bit. My dad thought I was crazy, but to me this was the ultimate. I used to drive around town thinking I was Dick Harriman.

"But I wasn't into the hot rod thing yet. I was more interested in having a cool-looking car. I was sixteen and going with my future wife, Lynn, and got this '55 Buick. Boy! Tuck and roll interior. Trick paint job. I painted it candy apple red. That was when candy apple first came out. That was a pretty nice car, but I traded it for a 27-T roadster* with no engine in it."

*A car based on a 1927 Model T Ford.

Snake bought a Buick V-8 engine for the car, drove it only a few times on the street, then took the engine out to put in a dragster body owned by a friend of his named Rod Pepmiller. They would take the car to the drag strip and take turns driving it. Prudhomme usually ran faster times than Pepmiller. The two belonged to a car club in Burbank called the Road Kings. One of the members was Tommy Ivo, a movie and television (*My Little Margie*) actor who also raced cars. One day Ivo told Prudhomme, "You know, you look better in that car than the other guy."

"That was the first compliment anybody ever paid me," Snake recalls.

In 1960 Ivo asked Prudhomme to accompany him as a crewman on an Eastern tour. Ivo towed his two-engine dragster behind a Cadillac limousine. "We would pull into drag strips in Illinois, Michigan, Pennsylvania, and people already knew TV Tommy Ivo. I thought that was amazing because I couldn't see beyond the Valley at the time. Here there were drag strips all over the country. All over the world. And Ivo was getting paid to race. I began to think that maybe someday I could be like him and become a professional racer."

Ivo was scheduled one weekend to race at Oswego Drag Strip near Chicago against Chris Karamesines, then the top-ranked dragster racer in the country. Karamesines planned a party at his home the night before the race and invited Ivo, adding, "Bring your guy along if you want."

"I couldn't believe it," Snake recalls. "Chris Karamesines! The Greek! He was my hero. I thought

Karamesines was God, and here I was actually going to his house. I was nervous as a cat. His wife, Marian, met us at the door, looked at me, and said, 'Oh, isn't he cute?' I turned three shades of red I was so embarrassed. I was the youngest one at the party. There was a guy at the bar, and he had a holster with a gun in it. Wow! After we left the party, I told Ivo how I thought Karamesines was the greatest, and Ivo said he was going to blow him off the next day. 'No way,' I said. Here I'm working for Ivo, and I'm telling him he's going to get beat. That didn't sit too well.

"So we went out to the track the next day, and Ivo actually beat him. I was really down, but a big thing happened. Ivo said, 'Why don't you make a run in the car?' Me? With Karamesines here and everybody? The Greek? Oh, my God. I was shaking just thinking about it. I got buckled into the car, and when I made my run, I ran almost as fast and quick as Ivo."

That was Prudhomme's only run while on tour. Later they visited an eighth-mile dirt track in the South. It began to rain, so Ivo permitted Prudhomme to steer the dragster while being towed back to the pits. "I was getting soaked. Mud was splattering off the tires until it was packed in my lap. But I didn't care, because I got a chance to sit in the car," he said.

Prudhomme returned to Southern California, bought one of Ivo's old dragster bodies, and raced it with his stock Buick engine. The car would go 140 mph. He met Dave Zeuschell, who had been building a 392-inch supercharged Chrysler engine. Prudhomme talked Zeuschell into putting the engine in his car and took it to San Fernando Drag Strip. *Voooom!* Prudhomme went 170 mph. He raced in March, 1962, at Bakersfield, California, against the top dragsters in the country—and won.

"I was brave back then," Snake recalls. "I had to be crazy to drive the stuff we drove then. We had no fire wall in the car. You'd be sitting there and look down at your feet, and all you'd see would be motor. If it caught fire, it would engulf you with flames. We didn't wear fire suits. I wore a leather jacket, leather gloves, a pair of goggles, and a face mask. Luckily we didn't have many fires then. Garlits had gotten burned, but we didn't pay too much attention to it.

"Then this guy from Kansas named Rod Stuckey came out to the Coast. He was running good. Kent Fuller built him a race car with a longer wheelbase and the engine tilted down. It was a kind of trick piece. Stuckey went out there and *Boom!* Beat all the guys. But he was running at Fremont one day when he blew an engine and got burned so badly he almost died. Everybody began getting worried. We decided to start sticking our pant legs down in our socks."

One day, while hanging around Tony Nancy's upholstery shop in Sherman Oaks, Don Prudhomme received a telephone call from Keith Black, a well-known builder of boat engines. Black wanted Snake to have lunch with him and Tom Greer, a wealthy machinery shop owner. When Don arrived at Black's shop, he found Keith lowering a new engine into a boat. "There were

Chrysler motors everywhere. All these parts and pieces. Before, I had been lucky to have even one engine. Greer arrived and we went to lunch. 'Here's what we want to do, kid. We want to make you a star.' Kind of like that. They offered me half of everything the car earned. I had been making 10 percent on my other car. 'Money's no object,' they said. I kept nodding my head and saying, 'Yes . . . Yes . . . Uh-huh . . . Yes.' I couldn't believe what was happening.

"The car got built, and it was real zippy and had a scoop on it. The first time out with the car at Pomona Drag Strip, a guy gave me a hole shot, jumped on me, but we drove around him and won anyway. The next week we went out and won, and the next week we won, and then we won, and then we won. It just kept on going." (During the 1963 and 1964 seasons, Snake would win more than 90 percent of his races driving the Greer, Black & Prudhomme dragster.)

"It was unbelievable how smart this Keith Black was. The car was ahead of its time. The other guys were building big engines with big strokes and using a lot of nitro. We ran almost a stock engine, but Keith was the first one to use a slipper clutch. I would leave the starting line, and the clutch would slip, allowing the car to move without smoking the tires. All the other drivers would nail the throttle. The clutch would lock, strike the tires, cause a lot of smoke, but they would hardly move. I'd win the race. This went on for the longest time, and I got cocky. I mean, I was God's gift to drag racing. I'm killing these guys. Nobody could beat me. Greer would give me a check, and before I could cash it I would have another one coming because we won week after week."

The National Hot Rod Association at that time refused to permit fuel-burning cars to run in their national championships. Don decided to marry his boyhood sweetheart, Lynn, the week of the Winternationals in 1963 and honeymoon in Hawaii. At the last minute NHRA lifted its ban, meaning Snake's car would be able to run. He got married anyway but returned from his honeymoon by the next weekend to win both ends of a weekend doubleheader at Lyon's Drag Strip.

Prudhomme had been operating as a part-time racer, working during the week painting cars at his father's body shop. Often he would stay up all night working on his race car and not get to work on time, so his father fired him. But by then he was making more money with his weekend hobby than with his regular job. Snake had also dropped out of high school, a touchy subject with him today. "I was only interested in cars," he admits. "Nobody could tell me anything back when I was that age."

A new drag strip was opening in Hawaii, and the Greer, Black & Prudhomme dragster was flown to the Islands for the event. It was on this trip that Don first met Roland Leong. "He was a young kid who wanted to get into drag racing. He was pretty bucks-up, but didn't know how to unscrew spark plugs yet. We became friendly. Roland owned an injected car that did all right, but he decided to build a blown Double-A fuel dragster. It was the most beautiful car you had ever seen: blue, sparkling, with the name 'Hawaiian' on the side. It was fantastic.

"We took it out to the drag strip, and Roland got in the car. He was so short that he could hardly see over the windshield. He brought the rpm's up on the starting line, let off the clutch, got about halfway down the track, decided 'Hey, you've got to steer one of these things,' and drove it off the side, over the railroad tracks, and into the weeds. Roland got out of the car so dazed he didn't know what happened. Couldn't even remember leaving the starting line. He decided that he didn't want to be a driver anymore and would just work on the car."

The Greer, Black & Prudhomme partnership, meanwhile, had begun to sour. Tom Greer wanted to quit drag racing to devote more time to his machinery business. Keith Black thought he deserved a larger percentage of the profits. Don Prudhomme wouldn't budge. So when Roland Leong asked Prudhomme to become his driver, Don agreed. "Roland wasn't afraid to spend money. Whatever it took, so needless to say, we were unbeatable. We went to the Winternationals in 1965 and won. That was my first major NHRA title, and it was one of the greatest thrills of my life," Prudhomme said.

"We went off on tour, the first time I had gone East since that time with Tommy Ivo. It was like my dream come true. The car, thanks to Keith, was set up perfectly. We were killers. We toured four months and got beat only twice, both times by the Ramchargers."

Prudhomme arrived at Indianapolis at the end of the summer to race in the Nationals and found he would have to face TV Tommy Ivo. The feud between the two former teammates had been growing, fueled by Snake's hot temper and Ivo's habit of playing pranks. Prudhomme had a garage behind his parents' house where he displayed his spare parts, hung from nails on the wall. It was a mechanic's art gallery. One day he received a phone call from McCourry and went into the house to answer it, leaving Ivo alone in the garage. Ivo took white paint and painted the backs of all the parts, rehanging them on the wall. Snake didn't discover the prank until several days later.

Once during a wrestling match, Prudhomme picked up Ivo, who only weighed around 120 pounds, and dumped him into a waste can. Later Don walked TV Tommy to his car. "See you later," said Don, and turned away, unaware that Ivo had hidden a bucket of oil on the seat next to him. "Hey, Don," called Ivo, and when Prudhomme turned around, he got hit in the face with the contents of the bucket. "That was his way of getting back at me," Snake explains. "I had oil all over me and couldn't see a thing, but I could hear him laughing as he fired his car and peeled away from the curb."

At a meet in Sacramento, Prudhomme returned to his motel room with Dave Zeuschell and found a beloved jacket that he had won in a race wrapped around a lampshade with pillow feathers filling the sleeves. "The whole room was a mess with shaving cream splattered all over," Snake remembers. Ivo was asleep next door. TV Tommy would carry blackout curtains with him and run a fan in the room to provide a constant hum so outside noises wouldn't bother him. Don and Zeuschell dumped the feathers into a wastepaper basket filled with oil. Prudhomme tiptoed into the hall carrying the basket.

Zeuschell, a burly guy weighing several hundred pounds, took a run at the door, knocking it off the hinges. TV Tommy sat straight up in bed, saying, "What the— " At that moment Prudhomme hit him in the face with the oil and feathers. "It went on and on like that between us," Snake claims.

The relationship between the two drivers became stormy only when Prudhomme began driving a car good enough to defeat that of TV Tommy. Ivo didn't like getting beaten by his former crewman. Prudhomme didn't like getting beaten by *anybody!* Even today he avoids mixing with other drivers. He stays at different motels. He eats alone or with his crew, rather than go out with the boys. His best friends are people he does not have to race against. While on tour back East, he often will climb on an airplane Sunday night and fly to California to spend a few days with his family rather than hang around with the other racers on tour.

"I like the fellows. I don't have anything against them, but I don't make a point of sitting around with them. A lot of guys think you should be over shucking and jiving all the time. I like to be alone at the races, and I would just as soon sit in my truck and relax. I don't want to talk to people. And if I'm beat, I'd just as soon leave the track. There have been many times when I've left with my fire suit on. The other drivers don't like that because they want you to sit around and face the music, so they can look at you and grin. My attitude is that if I don't win, I don't want to see anybody. Is that bad? That's the way I feel. I hope it rains and the race is over and nobody wins," Prudhomme says.

One summer Prudhomme was staying at a motel in New Jersey when he received a telephone call. It was TV Tommy Ivo, asking him if he would like to pick up $1,000 for a match race at a track in Islip, New York. "Fine," said Prudhomme. Drag racers actually can earn more money in match races than they can by winning championships. Usually two drivers will appear at a track for a match race and run against each other three times during a meet featuring mostly local cars. Each will get paid from $750 to $1,500 appearance money no matter who wins. It's like a preseason football game; it doesn't count in the standings. But most drag racers are such intense competitors that they hate to lose even races like these.

The track at Islip, however, was a 220-yard strip with a slowdown area so short that Ivo feared that one of them might get killed if they both raced to the lights. The two drivers agreed that they would race only partway and then lift off the throttle. Ivo also said that since he raced at this track all the time and was arranging the date, he didn't want to get beaten. Prudhomme grumbled over this arrangement, particularly since Ivo had been defeating him regularly all summer, but finally he agreed. In the first heat the two drivers left together, but Snake found himself unwilling to lift his foot off the throttle. He won the race.

At the end of the track Ivo confronted Prudhomme: "What's the big idea? We had an agreement."

"You don't need to win all three heats," Prudhomme snapped.

"I better win the next two."

"Yeah, yeah. I was wrong."

In the second heat an hour later, both cars left even again, but at half track Prudhomme lifted, allowing Ivo to pull ahead. TV Tommy had a muscular crewman named Tarzan who disliked Snake, and on the return road he leaned out of the truck window to sneer: "See, Prudhomme. Ivo can beat you any time he wants to!"

Ivo attempted to hush his crewman, but Prudhomme saw red. "I went smoking back to the pits and put 100 percent in it, did this, did that, and when I came up to the line next time, I was looking for blood," Prudhomme said.

But unknown to Snake, Ivo had talked with the starter. At the Islip track the starter would allow both cars to stage, wait four or five counts, and then turn on a green light. There was no automatic electrically timed countdown as there is today. "Listen," Ivo informed the starter, "our engines are getting too hot. The moment we stage, turn on the green light."

"Does Prudhomme know about it?" asked the starter.

"Yeah," said Ivo. "He's the one who suggested it."

The two dragsters did their burnouts, pulled up to the line, and at that instant Ivo left—just as the starter turned on the green light. Ivo won by a wide margin, but his parachute failed to open, and he skidded off the end of the track and into the parking lot before getting stopped. Ivo pulled off his helmet, saw Prudhomme approaching, and smiled, as if to say, "I told you this track was too short to race safely on."

Prudhomme, however, thought Ivo was smiling because he had beaten him. "That did it," Snake recalls. "I jumped out of the car, grabbed him, and had him bent backwards ready to punch him out when Tarzan pulled me off. There was a lot of name-calling, and I swore I'd never run at Islip again, and I haven't, although it wasn't the track's fault. I was really a hothead. Someone would hello me the wrong way, and I was ready to argue or fight."

Their big showdown, however, was at Indianapolis in 1965 with Prudhomme driving the Hawaiian fuel drag-ster. Under the qualifying setup then used at the Nationals, one finalist would be selected on Saturday, then would wait for Sunday's eliminations to produce a second finalist. Finally the two would make a single pass to determine the title of top eliminator.

Prudhomme won the Saturday trials, then had to spend a sleepless night worrying about whom he would race the next day. "I lay in bed thinking, *I hope it's not Ivo,* because he had been running well and might beat me. Sure enough, on Sunday it was Ivo. Even before Ivo's last run I had walked away from the car and sat down under a tree nearly a hundred yards away. I buried my head in my arms. I didn't even want to race, I was so nervous," he said. "I was actually shaking. Seriously, if I thought I could have hidden behind that tree all day and not have to race Ivo, I'd probably have stayed there. But this guy from Champion Spark Plugs, who had been around racing a long time, came over and told me to quit worrying, just to go out there and run him like anyone else.

"Finally I rose and climbed in the car and got buckled up, and they pushed me to the starting line. I refused to speak to Ivo before I got into the car. I didn't want him to know how nervous I was, so I asked Keith to flip the coin and decide the lane. Both cars came up to the line, and Ivo had this big smirk on his face. Keith had told me that he thought we'd win but to squat in my seat when I got down near the finish line because the car might explode. 'Great,' I said. 'I'm glad you've got it souped up.'

"So we came up on the line, staged, and the Christmas tree went blink-blink-blink, and I said go, caught it good, jumped into the lead over Ivo, held it all the way, beat him, ran the low e.t. of the meet, top speed, won the whole thing. Fantastic! I put Ivo away."

Ivo and Prudhomme continued to feud. TV Tommy complained to the press that Prudhomme was only as good as his machinery, that he was nothing, a junk driver, that if it weren't for the fantastic Hawaiian car, Snake never would have won. Prudhomme laughs about the feud now, admitting, "You know, he was right." The following year the Hawaiian car again won the Winternationals and Nationals—but with Mike Snively driving. "Ivo's comment kept eating at me, so I started learning more about engines, because some day I planned to have my own car in the winner's circle," Prudhomme said.

"How do you and Ivo get along now?" Prudhomme was asked recently.

"Actually we get along pretty good," he replied. "We don't race each other anymore. He's running the dragster and I'm running the funny car, so there's no longer any conflict between us." There is, however, conflict between Don Prudhomme and driver Tom McEwen.

"DON, TAKE ALL THE TIME YOU NEED, 'CAUSE I'M GOING TO MAKE IT RAIN"

The conflict between Don "the Snake" Prudhomme and Tom "the Mongoose" McEwen has resulted in the most profitable feud in racing history. The two have operated as partners, shared many of the same sponsors, and have parlayed their rivalry into a lot of money. Yet the feud is real and not merely trumped up for publicity purposes. A defeat by McEwen distresses Prudhomme more than a defeat by any other racer.

Prudhomme acquired the nickname Snake in the early sixties. "Joe Purcell, one of the guys in the crew, started calling me Snake," he explains, "because I was tall and thin and quick off the starting line. Everybody I would race, I would just *Bam!* Leave on them. So I was deadly—sort of. Plus my name is a little hard to pronounce, so soon the track announcers began to pick up on it. And the magazines. But I thought it was sort of phony and didn't like it at first. Except for Garlits, who was called the Swamp Rat, I was the only guy in drag racing with a name like that."

Then Tom McEwen came along, nicknaming himself after the mongoose, an animal in India that moves so quickly it can kill poisonous snakes. McEwen challenged Prudhomme to a match race at Long Beach Drag Strip. "That was his home track," Snake recalls, "and he studied it. They used to have an amber light, shut it off, and the green would come on. He would count one-two-three-GO! and hit it every time. He probably went up there at night and ran the lights. He was one of the first guys to leave like that. I always left on the green or when the flag dropped, because I was afraid of red-lighting. So the first round he left on me. I went quicker, but he beat me.

"I thought, that sucker isn't going to beat me again, so I left Greer and Black working on the car and went up to the starting line and practiced counting one-two-three-GO! one-two-three-GO! So the next race I counted one-two-three-GO! We both left together, and I beat him. But when we went up to the final round, he left even earlier. I went one-two-three and he was gone. The Mongoose beat the Snake.

"He called all the magazines and said, 'I'm the greatest,' and all this jazz. He started pushing this. And I'd call the magazines and say, 'This guy is crazy.' We started battling. We kind of liked each other, though, and started working together, figuring out ways to make money as a team until we got to be a team."

In 1969 McEwen and Prudhomme formed the Wildlife Racing Team, signing a contract with Mattel toys, which produced a line of Hot Wheel model race cars. Although still driving his dragster in championship races, Snake built a funny car for a series of match races against Mongoose. The toy company promotion soon implanted the names "Snake" and "Mongoose" on the consciousness of millions of small children, who would recognize the cars of the two rivals even though they might not recognize their faces.

Prudhomme pretends to dislike being bothered for autographs and pictures, but he is secretly pleased. In fact, it infuriates him if he thinks McEwen is getting as much attention as he does. After his victory at Tulsa in the National Challenge meet, Prudhomme discovered to his dismay that *Drag News* had published a picture of Tom McEwen on its cover. Snake picked up the telephone and berated the editor for his poor choice. The editor apologized, saying the cover had been planned long before the Tulsa meet. "Don't tell me that," Prudhomme barked. "You and McEwen are buddies. The two of you planned it just to irritate me. Don't ever use my picture on your cover again!" The following week the cover of *Drag News* contained a picture of Don Prudhomme, and the magazine later picked him as its funny car driver of the year.

The funny cars driven by Snake and Mongoose are almost identical, artistically speaking, except that the former is yellow and the latter red. At the end of the 1973 season, when the team lost their major sponsor, Care-Fee Gum, McEwen went out on his own and obtained the sponsorship of the U.S. Navy for the following year. Prudhomme learned of this and talked the U.S.

Army into sponsoring him, without telling McEwen or even his own crew. What delighted Prudhomme was that he felt he had obtained a better deal than his rival.

Several months after his showdown with McCulloch in the finals of the Nationals in Indianapolis, Prudhomme was to travel to Scottsdale, Arizona, for a funny car meet at Bee-Line Drag Strip. Most of the top drivers from Indy appeared: McCulloch, McEwen, Matsubara, Schumacher, and Nicoll. Two weeks earlier Snake had qualified for the Supernationals at Ontario Motor Speedway with a fantastic 6.16, two-tenths faster than his own NHRA record. McEwen had failed to make the sixteen-car field, as he had at Indy, but when rain caused a week's postponement, he replaced one of the drivers who couldn't compete. Prudhomme broke a rear end in the semifinals, and McEwen won the meet with a slowish 6.50. "He just backed into that win," Snake groused.

In the semifinals at Bee-Line, Prudhomme raced Jim Nicoll, who left on him, jumping to a three-car lead before Snake even hit the throttle. Still, Prudhomme almost caught him at the top end, setting a track record of 6.34. Nicoll ran only 6.70 while winning. Some observers thought the red light may have failed. But Nicoll damaged his engine, and so did McEwen in winning the other semifinal heat over Don Schumacher.

The time for the final came and went. Five minutes later McEwen finally got his car up to the line. Nicoll had his engine in pieces trying to make repairs. Another ten minutes passed, and Prudhomme, as first alternate, decided to tow his car to the line. Ed McCulloch and his mechanic had been working with McEwen, but the moment they saw Snake's car coming they jumped the fence to help Nicoll, who was still thrashing in the pits. Prudhomme climbed out of his car and walked over toward McEwen. "Let's not wait for Nicoll," he told him. "Why don't the two of us race?" McEwen frowned. His mechanic jumped the fence to help Nicoll.

Twenty minutes after the scheduled start, Nicoll completed his engine repairs and was towed to the line. Prudhomme waited in his car a few yards to the rear, ready to run should one of the others break. To avoid that, Nicoll and McEwen staged without a single burnout.

The light flashed green. Nicoll's engine threw a rod, and he spun off the track only fifty feet from the starting line. McEwen rumbled to victory, winning a full second slower than Prudhomme's semifinal time. Two days later Don and his wife had dinner with Billy Miller, a former drag racer, owner of a Sizzler restaurant, and one of Prudhomme's closest friends. Snake was still muttering about the loss: "They're all out to get me. They hate to see me win."

Miller nodded and described a television program about prehistoric man he had seen the night before. Man had been helpless against the animals as long as it was one man and one animal. Then man had discovered he could band together in tribes. A tribe of men could overcome a single animal by ganging up on him.

"That's the way it is with me and the other drivers," Snake complained. "They'll do anything to beat me. They'll blow up their engines. They'll leave early and take a chance on red-lighting. They just don't want me to win."

At the National Challenge meet in Tulsa, Prudhomme had faced Dale Pulde in the semifinals. Both cars prestaged, but neither driver would move the last eight inches to put out the second light. The heat of their engines rose to dangerous heights. Finally Snake staged, Pulde followed, and the green light flashed. Pulde broke on the line, however, and Prudhomme won—but he was burning mad.

He saw Pulde back in the pits. "You pull that trick on me again and you're going to get a shot in the mouth!"

"What do you mean?" Pulde flashed back. "That was my only chance. If you were in my shoes, you'd try anything you could to win."

Prudhomme walked off muttering to himself, but later he admitted with a grin, "You know, Pulde was right."

In 1966 Don Prudhomme had left the Hawaiian team, because he wanted to build his own race car and prove to TV Tommy Ivo and others that he could win on his own. At first it seemed a bad decision when the Hawaiian, with Mike Snively as its driver, won at the Winternationals and Nationals in 1966. Prudhomme teamed with Dave Zeuschell again to build a dragster that ran under the name B&M Torkmaster. Its gearbox was a forerunner of the two-speed gearboxes now used in all the professional drag race cars. It's good to be ahead of your time, but not too far ahead. Prudhomme's won/lost record was spotty.

The following year he drove for Lou Baney and won the Springnationals in Bristol, Tennessee, but Snake was still unhappy: "I was doing only half decent." In 1969 he talked the Wynn Oil Company into sponsoring him in a new dragster, which he named the Wynn's Winder. The company provided ample money, permitting Snake to buy the trick stuff (or good equipment) he felt he needed to race against the best. Most important, Snake now knew how to use it. Three things separate the top drivers from the also-rans: (1) talent, (2) money, and (3) experience. Don Prudhomme now had all three.

At this time Prudhomme employed a crew member named Donnie Neslund, a good worker unless a pretty girl walked by or somebody stopped to say hello. Then he sometimes forgot what he had been working on. Snake traveled to Martin, Michigan, one night to race the Beebe & Mulligan car. Neslund, interrupted while putting oil in the dragster, forgot to replace the oil filter plug. Prudhomme was pushed to the line without realizing this.

When he stabbed the throttle to make his burnout, a column of oil shot into the air like the gusher from a newly discovered oil well. The oil soaked Prudhomme. The officials attempted to push his car back, but he angrily waved them away. He figured he still might be able to make the run if he could find the plug. "If I could, I would have stuffed Neslund's hand down the oil pipe," Snake remembers. "But every time I hit the throttle to keep the engine running, more oil would blow out of the hole. All ten quarts were lying over me and the race car. Oh, was I mad."

Mulligan finally made a solo run, and Prudhomme shut off his engine. Then he saw Neslund standing beside the race car. He started to climb out ready to assault his mechanic, but the cockpit and roll cage were covered with oil. He'd pull himself halfway up and slide back down again, all the time shouting at the top of his lungs. "Funniest sight I ever saw," says McEwen. "He called Neslund every name in the books. He even brought his mother into it."

Prudhomme was runner-up at the Winternationals in Pomona, California, in February, 1969. Labor Day weekend he arrived at Indianapolis, hoping for another victory in the sport's most important race. Don Garlits had won at the Nationals the two previous years, but John Mulligan qualified with the lowest e.t.

In the first round, Garlits waited next in line as Mulligan raced TV Tommy Ivo. Suddenly the clutch exploded on Mulligan's dragster, causing him to crash in flames. (Two weeks later Mulligan died of the injuries he suffered.) After the wreckage had been cleared, Garlits staged to race Bennie Osborn, but was shaking so much from nervousness over Mulligan's accident that he bumped the mag kill switch, causing his engine to die. Meanwhile, Don Prudhomme progressed through the quarterfinals, although he had overstrained his engine.

Garlits visited Snake's pits before the semifinal round and glanced at his spark plugs. "This thing's hurt," said Garlits. "It won't make another run."

"Yes it will," Snake insisted. "We're going to win."

Prudhomme rolled up to the line to race Tom Raley with smoke pouring from one of his pipes. Veteran observers sadly shook their heads. Prudhomme defeated Raley anyway, but his engine let go in the lights. Garlits had ridden in Prudhomme's truck to the end of the strip. "I don't believe it, but you won," Garlits said.

"That's right, and we're going to win the next round," Snake snapped. Then he recognized the futility of his remark. "What am I saying? The engine's blown." Only forty-five minutes remained before the final round, and barring a miracle, there was no conceivable chance that he could change engines in that period of time.

At that moment it began to rain.

"The whole sky fell in," Prudhomme recalls. "I mean it was pouring. And I was cheering my head off. We went back to the pits, tore open the doors to our trailer, and I said, 'Anybody, everybody, help us change this motor!' So people started yanking our spare motor out of the trailer and screwing parts onto it, and half the guys didn't know how to take the headers off, much less change a motor. We had spectators rooting for us. They were holding a piece of canvas over the car to keep us fairly dry, but we were soaked, and they were soaked. The parts were hot, and it took us an hour and forty minutes, but we didn't have to be in line because it was raining. Oh, what a battle. Just when we got the last bolt on, it stopped raining. The sun came out, and click, it's dry.

"But we still had some disadvantages. The engine never even had been started before. We didn't know where to jet it. Roland Leong had been helping me since his car went out on the first round. He had gotten real good as a mechanic, and he understood dragsters. He said, 'You've come this far. Let's open the jets all the way.' We figured we've got one run to make, and we've got nothing to lose. We were racing Leland Kolb's car—Kelly Brown, the driver. I left good, and he left good, and ohhhhh, it was good! And Garlits and everybody else just fainted when my win light came on. For a year after I had to live down how lucky I was that it rained. It was as though the good Lord had said, 'Don, take all the time you need, because I'm going to make it rain.' McEwen claimed, 'It could only happen to Prudhomme.' But I always thought the harder you tried, the more breaks you got, and we tried hard, believe me."

Prudhomme returned to Indianapolis in 1970 and won again, matching Garlits' record of three victories. That final race has probably been seen by more people than any other drag race in history because of the resulting spectacular crash that has been replayed over and over by *Wide World of Sports*. ABC included the scene in its tenth-anniversary highlight show. It is probably one of the most dramatic moments ever shown on television.

Prudhomme met Jim Nicoll in the finals, and the two raced wheel to wheel to the finish line. Snake won by an uncomfortably narrow margin. Suddenly Nicoll's clutch exploded, hurling pieces of metal into the air like shrapnel from a grenade. The car was sliced in half, the front section caroming off Prudhomme's right front wheel. It is a grisly sight, as seen on television, just the frame and engine sliding in slow circles down the pavement, the camera following it, officials running to get out of the way, the twisted machinery clumping against the bales of hay at the end of the track—and no driver.

But the moment with the most dramatic impact is not the crash, but the picture of the agonized victor. Don Prudhomme stopped his car, looked at the twisted wreckage, and turned away in horror. The television camera caught him later sitting on one of the bales, head down, hands hiding his face. His wife, Lynn, bent over him. "I think I'm quitting," he told her, shaking his head. He looked up, and there were tears streaming from his eyes. "Oh, my god, I saw that car go by me. There was no back section on it or nothing," he said. Then Don Prudhomme stood up, pressed his hands against his temples, and walked away as though trying to escape the shadow of death.

Athletes—all athletes, but particularly automobile racing drivers—present a façade to the public. They wear a mask, when interviewed in public, that shows them as cool, calm individuals with no problems, no worries, no signs of nervousness, no fear. For that one moment that mask had been ripped from the face of Don Prudhomme and hurled to the ground.

But Nicoll had survived. The roll cage with him in it flipped over the guardrail. Nicoll was knocked out for a moment, but he walked away from the wreck. Three years later, before Don Prudhomme's dual with Ed Mc-Culloch at the Nationals, ABC telecaster Keith Jackson, asked Snake about the incident. The mask was back on Don Prudhomme's face now, and he was again the typical cool race driver. "I seriously thought at the time about quitting," he responded. "That was the first time in my drag racing career that I was racing a good friend of mine, and I figured he was dead at the time. Now what made me continue is that I really dig the sport. It's fantastic. But I think every race driver has thought about that from time to time, whether they admit it before a camera. They've been plenty shaken up."

Don Prudhomme claims that he is not afraid to race. After he had qualified at Indianapolis to meet Ed McCulloch in the finals of the Nationals, he was not even worrying about the dangers of his trade. He was more concerned with the problems of fixing the clutch in time for that last race.

4

"I'LL GIVE IT MY BEST SHOT"

Engine builder Ed Pink had watched the semifinal round while standing only a few feet from the starting line. As Prudhomme and Goldstein roared down the track, Pink observed carefully, rising on his toes to keep the cars in view as they rushed across the finish line a quarter mile away. When the light flashed next to Snake's lane, identifying him as the winner, Pink had relaxed for a moment. He then turned his attention to McCulloch and Matsubara as they approached the line.

Pink was attending the race not as a fan excited by the sound of thunder, but more like a doctor listening to the heartbeats of his patients. Don Prudhomme was a patient of Ed Pink, as was Ed McCulloch. Both drivers had their garages behind the Ed Pink Racing Engines Shop in Van Nuys, California. "Think Pink" was the motto of many drag racers. Eleven out of sixteen qualifiers in the Nationals used Pink engines. When McCulloch won the second heat, Pink smiled because both finalists were his clients.

Pink lifted the cap from his head and smoothed his long, silver hair with one hand. He stared straight ahead, squinting from the brightness of the sun. He was thinking. The engines of both finalists sounded good, but Snake had smoked his tires. Even if he hadn't seen the smoke, Pink's trained eye would have detected the wheel spin, because the Cuda's rear had lifted. This slight movement, caused by heat-swollen tires, would have gone undetected by all but the most knowledgeable fans sitting in the stands, but Pink knew Snake would have to readjust his clutch.

Pink replaced the cap on his head and began to walk to the funny car pits on the west border of Indianapolis Raceway Park.* He passed the booths with vendors selling hot dogs, Cokes, posters, and florid T-shirts. He passed the carnival tents where the parts companies showed their wares. He passed the section of the pits where contestants in the dozens of other NHRA classes worked on their machines. This area had been jammed with cars and mechanics the day before, but now, near the end of the Labor Day weekend, only the few finalists remained. Others had gone home or moved to the stands to become watchers instead of doers. Pink glanced at his watch and saw that it was nearly four. He spotted Darrell Zimmerman, the NHRA official who had charge of the pits. "How much time do we have?" Pink inquired.

*IRP actually is in suburban Clermont, about six miles west of the Speedway where the famous Indianapolis 500 is run each May.

"About an hour," said Zimmerman.

"We've got to do some work on Snake's car. Any time you can give us, we'd appreciate."

Zimmerman said he would see what he could do.

Pink arrived at Snake's work area at the same time as the truck towing the race car. The crew hopped from the truck and pushed the car onto the grass. Weasel slid a jack under the axle to lift the front end in the air. Jerry placed a pan under the engine to drain the oil. All twelve quarts must be dumped, because during a single six-second run, enough nitromethane fuel seeps past the rings and into the crankcase to foul the oil. Weasel spun a wrench, removing the spark plugs. They too would be thrown away after only one use, but not until they had been examined for possible heat damage. Weasel placed the plugs in a tray atop the supercharger, being careful to keep them in order. As he removed the spark plug from the number two cylinder, he frowned. Its electrode was badly burned.

Don Prudhomme had climbed out of the car near the tent used by Cragar Industries, the company that manufacturers the headers (or exhaust pipes) and racing wheels he uses on his car. He wanted to talk to Tom Shedden, a man whose opinion he respected, to ask how McCulloch had looked in his heat. Shedden had said he looked good. Now Prudhomme came striding swiftly up the road that was part of the sports car circuit for other races at IRP. He was blocked for a moment by two young boys: "Can we have your autograph?"

One of the differences between the sport of drag racing and other major professional sports is the ability of its fans to get close to the stars. A football fan who attends a game of the Miami Dolphins, for example, will see quarterback Bob Griese walk to the sidelines while the defense takes the field, but there is no way for that fan to approach Griese sitting on the bench. The football fan must stay glued to his seat in the thirty-fourth row. But a drag racing fan, by paying as little as $1 extra, can obtain a pit pass that will allow him to walk among the cars as they are being worked on and stand within a few feet of drag racing's major stars: Don Garlits, Ronnie Sox, Don Schumacher, Grumpy Jenkins, Gary Beck, Herb McCandless.

Furthermore, no football fan in his wildest dreams would ever think that he could stride onto a football field, assume the three-point stance, and line up next to Bob Griese. But at a drag race Don Prudhomme may make a pass in his funny car, covering the quarter mile in six seconds, and the next driver on the line may be a teenager driving a stock car that will cover that same distance in barely twenty seconds. Even at the Nationals, there were 1,300 entries, most of them amateurs, weekend racers, who once eliminated turn into spectators.

"People in the way," Don Prudhomme sometimes refers to them. "Like I wished none of them were there. Of course, the spectators are fine, but these people in the pits, everybody I look at, besides the crew that works on the car, are just people in the way. It's a bad attitude, I know, but that's the way I feel."

Nevertheless, at Indianapolis, Prudhomme paused long enough to sign autographs for the two boys, then walked quickly into his pits. "Where's that oil leak coming from?" he asked.

Jerry, head under the car, said he was checking.

Snake walked to where Ed Pink was awaiting him. "How does she look?"

"You're going to have to come up on the clutch," said Pink.

Prudhomme nodded as though he agreed. He turned to the truck where Wesel had placed the spark plug tray. "Take a look at number two," Pink suggested.

"Is it hurt?"

"Just fizzled a bit."

The heat in the 2,000-horsepower engine used to propel a funny car down the track must be carefully controlled. Too little heat, and the engine fails to produce enough power. Too much heat, and it will damage the engine. The amount of heat is controlled by the amount of fuel fed into the cylinders.

An engine can be run rich or lean. A rich mixture contains an excess of fuel. This will help cool the engine. Some of this excess fuel will still be burning as it is expelled out of the headers with the exhaust gases. When the funny cars run at night, you can tell if the engine is running rich by the flames roaring out of the header pipes. An engine running lean contains less fuel. At night the flames from the headers will form pencil-thin columns.

The hotter the engine, the easier the fuel will burn. This means more power, but also more heat. As a funny car moves down the track, the engine gets hotter, the fuel mixture leaner. If the heat grows too intense, it will melt a hole through the piston. Highly explosive nitromethane fuel will pour through the hole into the crankcase oil, and the result is an explosion and a serious fire. "We operate these engines on the razor edge of being lean enough to make power, but not too lean to burn up the engine," Ed Pink explained later.

Snake asked him, "Do you think we should change the piston?"

Pink picked up the burned spark plug and examined it with a magnifying glass, the way a doctor might examine an x-ray. "You're probably safe running with it." He handed the plug to Prudhomme.

Snake glanced at it and said, "Then let's pull the clutch."

Adjusting the clutch involved first removing a red-hot bell housing, but the task was routine. Drag racing crews perform in minutes complex mechanical adjustments that would take garage mechanics hours or days. There are several reasons why. First, they are used to working on the same car week after week. Secondly, the cars are built to be worked on. The bodies flip up, permitting easy access to parts. There are no radiators, batteries, or air conditioners, which get in the way of mechanics working on street cars. At another race I saw Snake's crew change engines between rounds, taking little more than an hour.

Wayne Hall, an NHRA pit official, arrived on a motor scooter. "How much time can you give us?" Snake asked him.

"How much time do you need?" Hall countered.

"We're going to pull the clutch."

"You're safe." Hall left to check with McCulloch at his pits.

Prudhomme seemed to relax. He didn't have time both to change a piston and to pull the clutch, but the decision had been made. Now he only had to do the work. He picked up a jug of ice water from the back of his truck and lifted the spigot to his mouth. The weekend before he had raced in the National Challenge, an American Hot Rod Association race in Tulsa, Oklahoma. It was hot, even hotter than in Indianapolis. He had won the finals, earning $25,000. To celebrate, Snake had poured a bucketful of ice water over his head.

He would have liked to have done the same now. He also would have liked to get something to eat. He had risen at six that morning and had eaten nothing since but some candy bars and Coke. He didn't eat more because it upsets his stomach. He was hungry, but he couldn't worry about being hungry, because he had one more race to run and was much too nervous to eat. "I couldn't swallow a hot dog if I had to while I'm in competition," he says. "But once you get beat, you don't have any trouble eating after that."

At Indianapolis Don Prudhomme set the jug of water back in the truck and used a rag to wipe his hands. Then he glanced up and noticed several spectators standing by the truck watching. People in the way. Prudhomme recognized a man named Stanley, who used to sweep the floor at Chris Karamesines' shop in Chicago, where he sometimes garaged his car while in the Midwest. Prudhomme paused long enough to shake hands with him, then returned his attention to Ed Pink, who held in his hand a sheet that listed results of the rounds run that day.

"How fast did McCulloch go?" asked Snake.

"He did a 6.48."

"He smoke the tires?"

"No."

"Yeah, that's what Shedden said too."

Pink left to talk with his other driver. Prudhomme walked to the side of the truck, where a rope, used to keep spectators away from the work area, lay on the ground. Snake picked up the rope and, using a piece of silver tape, attached it to the truck's fender. He thought of McCulloch doing the 6.48. For the first time he began to realize that he had the other driver beaten. "Aha, I've got him," he said to himself.

Snake's reasoning went this way: He had run 6.52 even though he had smoked his tires. McCulloch had run faster, but without smoking his tires. If Snake's clutch had worked properly, he would have run at least in the 6.30s. So all he needed to do was to adjust his clutch, run that fast, and barring some unforeseen problem, he should win.

Of course, drag racing is just a series of unforeseen problems, one after another. Thus Don Prudhomme's victory was far from assured.

5

"I SHALL FEAR NO EVIL"

After he had left Prudhomme's pits, Ed Pink walked farther down the road to where Ed Mc-Culloch was working on his car. The engine builder stood beneath the shade of the raised fiberglass body, examining spark plugs with a magnifying glass. Mc-Culloch waited by his side, a worried look on his face. "I don't see anything," said Pink.

McCulloch licked his lips with his tongue. He turned to his mechanic, Bernie Wadekamper, and pointed at the pan into which they had drained the crankcase oil. "Was that pan clean when you drained the oil into it?" Mc-Culloch asked.

Wadekamper said it was.

"You checked the main bearings?"

"They look okay."

McCulloch licked his lips again. He had defeated Billy Meyer in the opening round, smoking his spark plugs, a sign of bent rings. Because he had run the next-to-last heat in the first round and was scheduled to run the first heat of the second round, he had no time for major changes. He survived anyway, beating Bobby Rowe. Before his semifinal victory over Sush Matsubara, however, he had torn the engine apart, replacing five pistons. The engine had run well, but the oil pressure had been twenty pounds low. "If the oil pressure is down, it's got a reason for being down," McCulloch would explain later.

But he couldn't find a reason. None of the spark plugs hinted at any engine damage. The oil was clean. If the main bearings had been burned, the oil would have had a darker color to it. "Sometimes you can even smell the difference," McCulloch claims. The previous year McCulloch had met Connie Kaletta in the semifinals with oil pressure near zero but had won that round anyway and later took the championship. There was little he could do now about the lowered oil pressure, but it worried him.

Other decisions needed to be made, however. "What are we going to do about the clutch?" he asked Pin.

"What do you want to do?"

"Well, we could take some weight off."

"I don't think so," said Pink.

"Would it be better to tighten it back up?"

"That's what I would suggest."

McCulloch turned to his mechanic. "Bernie, let's pull the can." (By "can" he meant the bell housing surrounding the transmission.) They would be performing the same adjustments to their car as would the crew of Don Prudhomme.

McCulloch's crewmen began to lay out the tools necessary to do the mechanical work. "It's going to be the roughest part of the day," one said to another.

While his crew prepared his car, McCulloch went to the back of his truck and picked up a plastic cup full of ice water. He drank the water in one gulp. Wayne Hall, the NHRA pit official, arrived on his motor scooter to ask, "How does it look?"

McCulloch slowly shook his head, as though he thought they would never make it to the starting line. "We're changing the clutch, and we're going to need some extra time."

"Ed, just as soon as you get her ready," said Hall, then motored off.

McCulloch leaned against the side of this truck and watched as his crew began unbolting pieces from his car. There was an air of silent panic in the McCulloch pits, but he knew that when it came time to go to the line, he would be ready.

Several years before, he had changed an engine before meeting Dale Pulde in the finals of the Nationals.

"They were sitting at the line screaming to run," he recalled later. "They wanted to sail, and here we were still thrashing in the pits. Going to the starting line, we were still bolting pieces onto the car. We beat them anyway. Last year at Ontario, I was running Pat Foster in the third round. We had all the pistons out, having changed the rings, and they were calling us to the starting line. They had run the first two cars. I heard them racing. The officials were saying, 'Okay. Everything's okay.' I was suiting up and getting into the car, and they still didn't have it all together. I mean, we didn't even have the spark plugs in it."

McCulloch had lost that race. "You have to keep the official guys on your side," he explains. "If you need an extra five or ten minutes, they can fake it for you. By checking with them, you involve them in what you're doing, and it seems to help."

McCulloch tipped the plastic cup to his mouth again, obtaining a few more drops of melted ice water. A trailer carrying the Ramchargers funny car passed on its way out of the track. With only two cars remaining in the field, most of those eliminated already had put their cars back on the trailers and were leaving to beat the traffic rush. Several friends stood near where McCulloch leaned against the truck, but he did not talk to them, and they did not talk to him. "I don't get nervous anymore," he says, "but sometimes I'm very irritable, very edgy. People that come up who don't really know me probably think they don't like me, because when I'm competing I'm thinking of the race.

"You've got to be emotionally up to drive a race car. Just like a football player has got to get up to play a football game. A football team that parties around won't play well the next day. You've got to get mentally ready to do what you're going to do. That's just an old piece of steel with some fiberglass over it, and it shouldn't know any difference, but your attitude has got more to do with it than a lot."

Ed McCulloch was born in Vasalia, California, in 1942. His parents moved to a farm outside Portland in

1961, and Ed went with them to help farm 1,800 acres. Racing became a hobby. He drove gas dragsters and later fuel dragsters. The top area driver then was Jerry Ruth, who billed himself as King of the Northwest. McCulloch beat Ruth several times, and a sportswriter from Bremerton, Washington, wrote a story saying, "What beats a King? An Ace." The nickname Ace stuck.

In 1969 a friend named Art Whipple built a funny car, and the two joined to form the Whipple and Mc-Culloch team. They soon sold that car plus McCulloch's dragster and used the money to build a still-better funny car. McCulloch became the first West Coast driver to break seven seconds in a funny car when he ran 6.97 seconds at Seattle International Raceway. The time earned him a $1,000 bonus prize. He set NHRA records for both e.t. and top speed in 1970 and planned to bring his racer to Indianapolis for the U.S. Nationals over the Labor Day weekend. But while driving to Seattle for a car show, Mc-Culloch suddenly saw smoke in the rear-vision mirror. An electrical short circuit had set the trailer on fire. Whipple and McCulloch lost their car, their clothes, and all their equipment.

The following year he did race at Indianapolis, winning his first national championship. In February, 1972, he also won the Winternationals at Pomona, California. McCulloch would win four different "national" races in 1972, an accomplishment unmatched by any other driver, but he still had problems.

That spring, while racing Mark Higginbotham in West Palm Beach, Florida, a crankshaft broke, blowing the engine out of his car, ripping off the fiberglass top, and cutting the car in two. McCulloch skidded off the track to the right, his goggles so covered with oil that he couldn't see. A piece from his blower belt also flew into the next lane, lodging on the throttle linkage of Higginbotham's car. Higginbotham shot off the end of the strip, his throttle jammed open. "He was on fire at the end, and my car was scattered about everywhere," McCulloch would recall. "It was just sort of a big mess." But neither driver was seriously injured.

A sign on the wall of Ace McCulloch's Van Nuys garage says: "Yea, though I walk through the valley of the shadow of death I shall fear no evil—for I am the meanest dog in the Valley."

McCulloch returned to Indianapolis later that summer to achieve his second victory at the U.S. Nationals, even though his blower belt flew off the car at the end of his final run. He and his mechanic and partner, Ed Whipple, had parted company by then, but not from any disagreement. Whipple had gotten married and wanted to stay home with his new wife, rather than spend each summer following the drag racing circuit of match races three and four times a week and every night a new motel. "Drag racing is my life," claims McCulloch. "I enjoy it. It's hard, but it's my way of making a living. It would be nice to get on top, relax, and just retire, but that's not my way. You have to continue to run to the best of your ability wherever you go."

But as he watched the work progress on his car, Ace McCulloch felt uncomfortable about his chances for victory. He looked tired, and his car looked tired. Its fiberglass body showed wear. It was tarnished. Small cracks marred the finish. Heat from the headers had blistered the sides, obscuring in some places the name RRRRRRRRRREVLLUTION! (Revell, a toy company that makes model race cars, was his major sponsor.) "I had qualified with a 6.42, then had run 6.40, 6.40, and 6.48," McCulloch said later. "I was running consistently, but not quick enough. I felt that I should have been running a tenth faster. I hadn't slipped backwards, but I also hadn't progressed as much as I should have. Our combination was not quite right. We had had quite a bit of breakage during the year. When a car is running well, it will drive smooth and won't hurt many pieces. But when you're confused, trying this and that, hunting and scratching, you use up a lot of parts. When you're on top, there's only one way you can go: down. The ladder is only so high, and every time you win a major event, your chances of winning the next one are just that much slimmer. But I've won a lot of national meets, and you figure that if you can just get into the last round, you are no worse than runner-up—and that's not bad."

McCulloch tipped the plastic cup again, letting the last few pieces of ice slide into his mouth. He began cracking them with his teeth, continuing to stare ahead, watching the work progress on his car, and saying very little.

6

"PLASTIC-BODIED REPLICAS OF DETROIT IRON"

Back in Don Prudhomme's pits, the ropes that he had carefully taped to the truck fender already had fallen to the ground, but few people were present to invade his work area. Most fans had abandoned the pits in favor of the grandstands as the day neared its climax. The photographers had also left to take positions around the drag strip. Only a handful of onlookers watched as Snake poured fuel from two large square plastic containers into the fuel tank between his car's front wheels. He next inserted a hose into the tank, connected it to a longer length of hose that ran into his trailer, and turned on the spigot. Clear liquid splashed out of the tank as it overflowed.

The fuel used by funny car drivers is highly explosive nitromethane (what had been in the two plastic containers). This is diluted by adding methanol, a type of alcohol that is burned in cars that race in the Indianapolis 500. Indy drivers sometimes use nitromethane, but only for short qualifying runs, and then only in small percentages. If they used nitromethane during a race, they would risk blowing their engines to bits.

But since drag racers have only 1,320 feet to drive, they "tip the can," sometimes using a mixture that is nearly all nitro, the rest prayer. At Indianapolis Prudhomme was using a 90 percent mixture. After filling his tank, he siphoned some fuel out into a glass beaker and tested it with a hydrometer. Each percentage point is critical. If he were to allow the percentage of nitro vs. methanol to drop to 88 percent, it might mean the difference between running 6.42 seconds instead of 6.38. If he were to allow the percentage to rise to 92 percent, he might explode the engine.

What complicates the process further is that the percentage can change depending on the temperature or the humidity. "It's like running along the top of a fence as fast as you can without falling off to one side or the other," says Snake. He examined the hydrometer floating in the beaker and saw that it registered right at 90 percent. He dumped the fuel from the beaker back into the tank and put his chemistry set back on the truck.

A passerby announced, "McCulloch's tore down. He's working on his clutch." Snake didn't respond to the information, although he stored it in his mind for future use. At a later time he might want to know the condition of his rival's car. At this moment he was more concerned with getting his own ready to run. He stood and gazed around him at the sky. It was clear and cloudless.

"I'm like a weatherman," he later explained. "I'm constantly watching cloud formations. A lot of guys don't do that, but it's a practice with me. Clouds bring dampness with them. As they get closer, the air density changes. I have a humidity gauge, and you can watch it rise. When that happens, your fuel mixture changes, because the air intake sucks in the moist air. This can be very critical in the performance of the engine, especially in the Midwest and especially at night when you can't see the clouds. The only way you can tell is by the gauge. It's an advantage when you learn to use one; it's part of running the race car. Even when I've got my fire suit on and am sitting in the car, I'll look at the gauge, and we may make a jet change the last second before we run."

Jerry, who had been lying on his back beneath the engine, rose to announce, "That oil leak was from a loose gasket."

"You fix it?"

"Right."

Prudhomme said nothing; he merely frowned. It was enough of a frown to indicate to his crew that he was merely displeased, not angry. When Snake becomes angry, he explodes with a fury barely matched by the roar of his engine, and he easily could have vented that anger now. A single bolt carelessly left untightened could cost him the race—or even his life.

He expects high standards from his crewmen because he set high standards as a mechanic himself when he crewed for TV Tommy Ivo. "I was a good helper," says Snake. "When Ivo was working, he would say, 'Give me a nine-sixteenths,' stick out his hand, and a nine-sixteenths would drop into it. Like a surgeon being assisted by a nurse. That's the way Weasel is, and that's the way Jerry is, and that's the way it's got to be. If you go for a bolt, your guy should see you going for it and hand it to you."

Prudhomme detests carelessness. Jerry Herrier could have offered as excuse the fact that the gasket bolt had been left untightened by one of the guest crewmen helping them. But excuses are only for losers, so nothing was said. Besides, it was too hot.

Snake walked back to the truck, picked up a cup of lemonade, and drank. He wiped his brow with the sleeve of his T-shirt. He moved back again toward the car. "Where's that five-eighths socket?" he asked.

Meanwhile, back on the track, cars in lesser classes were making their final runs. There are two basic categories at the Nationals: Group I and Group II.

Group I is the *professional* category, the classes where the prizes and spectator interest is highest. It consists of:

1. Top fuel
2. Funny car
3. Pro stock

Group II is an *amateur* category, designed mostly for part-time racers. It consists of:

1. Competition
2. Modified
3. Super stock
4. Stock

There are twenty-six classes of modified cars, forty classes of super stock, and forty-eight classes of stock cars. The competition category contains a grab-bag mix of cars competing on a handicap basis. There also is a category for motorcycles. The total of championship classes thus is 116, and it is little wonder that sports reporters, used to covering the World Series or Super Bowl where only one victor emerges, return to their desks shaking their heads in wonder and confusion.

But the key to understanding the Nationals is that the big money is spent in Group I, the three professional categories. Pro stocks are standard, gasoline-burning Detroit automobiles, which have been hopped up to the absolute limit. Bob Glidden of Greenwood, Indiana, the winner in that class, was to go the quarter mile in 9.085 seconds and 151.26 mph.

The appeal of pro stock cars is that they are the fastest breed among the so-called stock (or factory) automobiles. The fan who sits in the stands can identify most closely with them. And he can believe that if he had $30,000 (the going price for a top pro stock machine) to invest, he could be down there racing the champions. Pro stock cars are exciting to watch. They approach the starting line as jungle animals might. They snarl; they shake; they lunge. Then with a mighty roar, they rush off down the track.

The fuel dragster is the most radical machine raced at a drag strip, with its long, rail-like body and tiny front wheels and a massive engine cradled by two giant tires behind. The drivers, clearly visible in their cockpits, dress in bulky fire suits, masks, and helmets, which add to the surreal atmosphere. They are the fastest regularly raced class. The winner at the U.S. Nationals, Gary Beck of Edmonton, Canada, would cover the quarter mile in 6.047 seconds, going 243.9 mph. If pro stock machines may be compared to jungle animals, then dragsters may be compared to arrows. They sit on the starting line pointed down the track as though cocked in some archer's bow. Then: *Flick!* They're gone, almost flying toward the target.

But the crowds come to see the funny cars, "the plastic-bodied replicas of Detroit iron" (as the track announcer would describe them). They are a blend of the other two professional classes: fuel dragster frames onto which a fiberglass body has been dropped.

When funny cars developed in the mid-sixties, they were more like today's pro stocks: funny mostly in that they had mismatched engines and bodies. For example, a Chrysler engine might be used to propel a Ford car. Then the breed grew wilder. In their never-ending quest for speed, funny car mechanics developed tubular chassis just like the dragsters. They started using fiberglass hoods and fenders to lighten their cars and soon developed flip-top bodies that weighed only 100 pounds. If pro stocks are animals and dragsters arrows, then funny cars are creatures from outer space.

Each class of competition has its own sound, a certain pitch, so you could blindfold an experienced mechanic and he still could tell you what class car was on the track. But you need not be a mechanic to recognize the roar of the funny cars as they approach the starting line. It is a sound louder than anything else that races at a drag strip:

RUMMMP!
crackle-crackle-crackle
RUMMMP!

Dragsters have exhaust pipes mounted atop the engine, and the sound rises from the engine up. But funny cars have exhaust pipes curling downward, and the sound rises from the *ground up*!

Even while idling, funny cars have a low-pitched, gargling, crackling, almost funky sound, like a lot of little firecrackers going off into a loudspeaker. But most impressive is their full-throttled roar, a hot-breathed shout, and the suddenness with which it attacks your eardrums: YAHHHHHHHHHH! The sound strikes like a scream of anger; then as quickly as it came, it moves away from you down the track. So powerful are the funny cars that even at 230 mph going through the lights, they are still laying down rubber, clawing at the ground, spinning their tires, trying to hook up to the pavement.

And they are expensive. A person wanting to become a funny car driver can spend up to $25,000 to buy or build his racing machine, will need at least that much in parts and equipment, and will spend another $25,000 in salaries, travel cost, and other expenses for a year of racing. A clutch that will last forty runs cost $400. A supercharger will make about the same number of runs; it cost $800. Engines sell for $8,500 and last a hundred runs—maybe! Rear tires cost $170 a pair; six to ten runs and they are history. Spark plugs ($2 a piece for a set of eight) must be thrown away after each trip down the track. A dozen quarts of special racing oil ($20 for a case of twelve quarts) also gets dumped. Nitromethane fuel costs $7.50 a gallon, and five to eight gallons get burned each pass.

Because Don Prudhomme has sponsors who provide him with plugs, oil, tires, and other parts, his visible expenses for a single run down the drag strip would come to around $40 (the cost of the nitro). But a race promoter who came to him and offered him that much money for one more run down the strip would get turned down quickly. There are many invisible expenses, such as wear and tear on parts and equipment, plus salaries and expenses of the crew. Don Schumacher, winner of the funny car class at the Nationals in 1970, runs three cars and has a $750,000 racing budget. Averaging out all expenses, he figures that each time he climbs into his car it costs him $300. The costs for even a low-budget funny car would amount to at least $150 a run, and low-budget cars win very few national titles.

The amount of money a drag racer can earn is limited. Depending on his reputation, he can command between $750 and $1,500 for a day's work, which usually consists of three runs down the track.

When you consider expenses, the profit margin is thin. A blown engine may wipe out a month's profits; a crash or fire may cancel profits for a year. At U.S. 30 Drag Strip near Gary, Indiana, a few weeks before the Nationals, the Blue Max, driven by Richard Tharp, burst into flames as it passed through the lights. Tharp had to be pulled from the flames by Tom McEwen, who was racing in the next lane. After the fire department had extinguished the blaze, Tharp came walking back to the starting line, his fire suit covered with soot, his face ashen, his eyes glazed. It was partly because he had stared death in the face, but also because the accident had turned his $20,000 racing machine, his livelihood, into a pile of twisted rubble that even a junk dealer would scorn.

Although more than $351,000 in prizes were posted for the Nationals, most racers there probably spent more than they won. Yet a few top-ranking drivers do earn as much money as the stars in other sports. Don Garlits Grosses near $200,000 annually and after expenses keeps half that sum. Don Prudhomme and Tom McEwen each earn about the same.

The secret is sponsorship. The top drivers earn most of their money from sponsors who want to display their product on the sides of race cars or use drivers' names and faces for advertising. Don Garlits would be seen on TV commercials between innings of the World Series promoting Champion Spark Plugs. His dragster contains so many sponsor names that he almost needs a trailer to display them.

Likewise, Don Prudhomme had come to Indianapolis heavily mortgaged to sponsors such as Car-Free Gum (the doors), and Coca-Cola (the rear deck), and Wynn's Oil (the fenders). Wynn's, in fact, was displayed in six positions. By examining Snake's car, you could learn that he also used Cragar Wheels, Pennzoil, Lee Batteries, Lenco Racing Transmissions, Bell Helmets, Simpson Safety Equipment, and more. The following year there would be a new mix of stickers as sponsors changed.

Prudhomme is as shrewd a businessman as he is fast as a driver. He knows who pays his salary. A reporter once asked him what he was drinking at a drag meet. "Coca-Cola," Snake replied.

But the reporter said the drink in his hand looked as though it might be lemonade. "Coca-Cola," Snake insisted with a smile. "I sometimes even have it for breakfast."

"Did you hear how Snake got so tight with Goodyear?" McCulloch comments. "He was being interviewed a couple of years ago on television. He jumps out of the dragster, and the announcer asks him, 'To what do you attribute your great win?' Snake reaches back and puts one hand on the rear wheel and answers, 'My Goodyear tires.' I'll tell you, that made him a millionaire."

But that was 1970, when Don Prudhomme had won his third victory at the Nationals driving a fuel dragster. Since that time he, and many of the other top dragster drivers, had switched to funny cars. The main reason was that it was easier to obtain race dates and sponsor money while driving in that category. The sponsors liked the cars better because there was more room on a funny car to display their product names. And they noticed, along with track promoters, that the grandstands would fill just before the finny cars ran and begin to empty the moment the last of that breed went through the lights.

"What would you rather drive: a dragster or a funny car?" Don Prudhomme was asked once.

"I get asked that quite a bit," he responded. "It's a tough question, you know. The dragsters are fastest, so you get satisfaction from that. But while running at Indy, we ran 231 mph and did it in 6.27 seconds. Well, that's flying no matter what you're in.

"I enjoy the funny cars more. If I had to choose between driving a dragster or a funny car, I would have to take the funny car. Now the reason for that is it's more pleasing to the spectators. You can go out and run fast, and they really like it. They think: *Wow! That's really something.* You can go out and run 6.05 in a dragster, and they say, 'Oh, that's nice.'

"Driving a funny car is every bit as hard as driving a dragster. In most cases, it's harder. The car is more difficult to sort out. The competition is tougher. We go to these sixteen-car shows back East at smaller tracks like Martin, Michigan. The Chitown Hustler, Schumacher, McEwen, McCulloch, you name it. There are sixteen of the baddest funny cars in the world, and you've got to go out and try to blow those guys off. You run your car there as hard as you would at Indianapolis.

"To the real racers, dragsters are more important, because they can appreciate a car going 5.95. I can appreciate that. But week in, week out, with something to make you a living, a funny car keeps you going a bit more. The sponsors like them. If I were running my dragster next year, I would have as many sponsors, but not some of the other guys.

"Sitting in the grandstand, I would rather watch the funny cars. I mean, there are a few dragsters I like to watch. I like to watch Garlits run. I always enjoy watching him—and one or two others. But I enjoy watching just about any funny car. They are exciting."

If Don Prudhomme could win the funny car championships at the Nationals, not only would he become the first four-time winner, but he also would become the first top driver to win titles in more than one professional class at the National Hot Rod Association's premiere event. NHRA had been founded in 1951 by Wally Parks as a means to get drag racers (then popularly known as hot rodders) off the public streets and onto safe tracks. In 1955 NHRA established a major championship meet at the municipal airport at Great Bend, Kansas. This event, which became known as the Nationals, moved in later years to Kansas City, Oklahoma City, and Detroit before finding a permanent home at Indianapolis Raceway Park. The six-day meet, held over the Labor Day weekend, now attracts more than 100,000 spectators each year.

As drag racing grew in popularity, other organizations appeared, among them the American Hot Rod Association and the International Hot Rod Association. Each sponsors so-called national championships. During a single calendar year, NHRA itself sponsors eight "national" meets, including the Summernationals, the Gatornationals, and even the Supernationals. But despite this obvious overuse of the term "national championship," there never was any question in any true drag racer's mind on which event was the biggest and best of the year. According to the program for the Nationals:

> While winning any of NHRA's eight scheduled national meets is always a most memorable moment in any drag racer's career, there is still

nothing that can quite match the thrill and pride that comes with a victory at the U.S. Nationals, the sport's premiere championship event. . . . What is perhaps closest to the hearts of the campaigners is just the fact of knowing that they have won the biggest and most competitive race of them all, and in the process have earned the unchallenged respect and admiration of their fellow racers. Winning the U.S. Nationals means that you are the best, that you are number one, and no one will have a chance to dispute that fact until the next event rolls around one year later.

Don Prudhomme agrees with this—to a point. "I can remember," he recalls, "when a guy would win the Nationals and book his car the rest of the season from that win. Nowadays it isn't that way. You can win the race, and you'll get some dates and a lot of publicity, but there are so many races now that it doesn't mean that much anymore. Next week there's another big race and another new champion. That's the pity of the whole thing. There's nothing you can do about it, so winning the race is only as important as you make it."

"But there are other reasons why drag racers want to win at the Nationals," a friend suggested.

"Ninety percent of the guys are out there at the Nationals because it's the thing to do," Snake replied. "Not too many go there thinking, *Boy, if I win this race, I'm going to have me some big sponsors next year, and I'm going to get all kinds of dates.* Those days are gone. In my eyes, they go out there to prove themselves and to prove to the other racers that they are the baddest guys in town. You get to Indy with all those people in the stands, all those cameras focusing on you, and beat the world. The other stuff comes secondary."

"It's the prestige," the friend suggested.

"Prestige, yes, but—"

"Being king of the mountain."

"Yeah," said Snake. He laughed and slowly shook his head. "But they forget fast. They forget fast."

7

"JUST STAB THE THROTTLE
AND GO IN A STRAIGHT LINE"

A s work on Don Prudhomme's car continued and it became apparent that he would face no major problems in preparing for the final round, he relaxed. The anger, so apparent earlier, had subsided. When Ed Pink returned from McCulloch's pits, Prudhomme greeted him with an impish grin. "Congratulations," Snake said.

"What for?" asked Pink.

"Well, you've won, haven't you?"

Pink looked puzzled, then realized Prudhomme was referring to the fact that both finalists used Ed Pink racing and engines. The two men laughed, but it would be nearly another hour before Don Prudhomme would discover whether or not he could celebrate a personal victory.

Drag racers, particularly winning ones, never have trouble obtaining extra help at a race like Indianapolis. Mechanics from defeated cars often shift to the machine that beat them. They hope to share in the final victory, but there is also a natural tendency among competitors at drag races simply to be of help. Though sworn enemies on the track, they give freely of parts, tools, and time while back in the pits.

It is like the barn raisings that occurred in pioneer days. The neighbors would gather on a weekend to build someone a barn, partly because it was fun to do things together, but also because they knew someday they might want help in building their own barn.

Thus Steve Montrelli, a crewman for the already-defeated Don Schumacher, helped Ed McCulloch prepare for the finals. (Three weeks later, at another race, Montrelli was to assist Don Prudhomme change a blown engine.) At Indianapolis Snake had Steve Bernd helping him. Bernd, better known as Okie, once had worked with Snake but now crewed for Tom Prock. Prock's car had been eliminated, so now Okie was helping Snake. Also helping were two employees of Ed Pink, Bob Wesphal and Art Christman; Ed's son, Billie Pink; Alan Earman, a freelance photographer; Jim Irving, whose brother worked as one of Don Schumacher's mechanics; and ten-year-old Richard Marantette. "Richard provided moral support," Prudhomme recalled. "He wore our shirt, and every time I looked at him he'd give me a big grin."

Billie Pink and Steve Bernd took charge of repacking the parachute. The two carefully stretched out the lines, folded the canopy into foot-wide squares, laid the lines on top, then cautiously tucked this bundle into a canvas holder on the rear of the car. This package finally was secured with elastic laces. During a run down the drag strip, Prudhomme would yank the parachute lever even before reaching the first timing light. By the time he reached the second light, the chute would pop open.

Drivers can halt their cars without use of the chute simply by standing on the brakes. The parachute offers an extra margin of safety and can prevent excessive brake wear. Sometimes the chute will fail to open. "It's not as bad as when you're jumping from an airplane," says Prudhomme, "but it's bad. You can crash, so I make sure that baby is blossoming in the last light. If it doesn't, I'm on the brake as hard as I can get. I'd stick my feet out and start dragging them if I had to."

One of the first drivers to employ a parachute on his car was TV Tommy Ivo at the time he was driving two- and even four-engined race cars, because the cars were heavy and their brakes poor. Ivo first employed a chute similar to the kind used for landing jet aircraft on short runways. "It was so stout," Prudhomme recalls, "that you'd pull the ripcord, and it would practically throw you backwards over the finish line." Eventually drag racers began cutting holes in the chutes and then modifying them specially for racing. The ones in use today are more similar to those used for landing cargo than to the kind you jump out of an airplane with. They have to be specially engineered for the weight of the car and its speed. "If I started running 250 mph with my funny car, the parachute wouldn't be efficient enough," says Snake. "I'd tear it to bits."

The parachute on Don Prudhomme's Cuda usually is packed neatly, almost tenderly, by mechanic Bob Brandt, the Weasel. Weasel takes extra care to assure the chute's proper functioning because he doesn't want to lose his driver. Sometimes, when time is short, Prudhomme will pack the chute himself, his method being to just cram it, unfolded into the canvas holder. "Don't worry. It'll work," he then assures Weasel.

"Do you want me to pack it your way next time?" Weasel asks.

Snake smiles. "No, just continue the way you always do."

But as the time for the final run approached, there was little sense of panic in the Prudhomme pits. The machine-gun-like rattle of the electric impact wrenches signaled that the clutch assembly was nearly back together. The heavy sixty-weight racing oil, twelve quarts of it, was being poured through a funnel into the engine. The climax of five day's work was only minutes away.

Weasel and Jerry, Prudhomme's two regular crew-mean, had arrived in Indianapolis on Thursday, having driven 641 miles from Tulsa where Snake had raced the weekend before. They were a day late, having remained in Tulsa to fix a wheel on their trailer. They passed the car through technical inspection that afternoon. (Before any car can run at the Nationals, it must pass a strict inspec-tion to ensure it conforms to NHRA rules, most of which relate to safety.)

They spent some time straightening a front axle at the Hurst machine shop. Unlike the Indianapolis Motor Speedway some six miles to the east, IRP has no permanent garages. Few drag strips do. Drag racers are used to functioning like campers, staking out a plot of ground and working from the backs of their trucks and trailers.

After picking a place for their pits, Weasel and Jerry set the burglar alarm on the trailer containing the funny car and went to the Roadway Inn, where they were staying, to shower, eat dinner, and go to bed. Because of the security guards, they felt their equipment would be safer at the track than at the motel, where it would be unguarded once they fell asleep. Drag racers are constantly being preyed on by car thieves. A few weeks earlier, driver Grumpy Jenkins stopped to have lunch at a restaurant near St. Louis, leaving the car carrier with his pro stock racer parked in front. When he came out a half hour later, it was gone. Police later found the car minus engine and running gear.

In 1971 Snake had left Indianapolis in a rush by air, furious at being eliminated in the first round. He was asleep back in Granada Hills the next morning when a jangling telephone awakened him. Without getting out of bed, he reached for the phone. It was Bill Hermes, his mechanic, calling from Indianapolis. "I've got some bad news for you," said Hermes.

"What possibly could you tell me worse than what's happened already," Snake grumbled.

"Your truck has been stolen."

Prudhomme later said he thought he was having a nightmare and simply dropped the phone back on the cradle. A minute later Hermes called back to tell him it was true.

Several weeks after Snake's race at the Nationals with McCulloch, burglars cut a hole in the fence around Ed Pink's shop, drove their truck through, and loaded it with $8,000 worth of Prudhomme's tools and parts. This time Snake was in Akron, Ohio, talking with executives at Goodyear about sponsorship for the coming season. Furious, he climbed on the first plane for home. A few days later he learned through the grapevine the probable identity of the thieves. Accompanied by his brother, his crew, and several strong friends, Snake walked into the suspected burglars' garage one evening. He was carrying a baseball bat, but he hadn't come to play baseball. The burglars denied any knowledge of the theft.

"What's under that canvas?" snapped Snake.

"Nothing, man. Nothing," pleaded one of the burglars.

Prudhomme lifted the canvas and found a portion of his stolen gear. "After that the scene got pretty bad," Weasel recalls. "As a matter of fact, it got so bad that the burglars wound up calling the police."

At the Nationals Snake had flown into town late on Thursday. Friday he made two runs, clocking 6.68 and 6.60 seconds. On Saturday he changed the cam in his car and ran 6.42, then the second-fastest time. After some minor adjustments, he hit 6.41 even though smoking the tires. "That impressed us," Weasel would recall. "We decided to come back Sunday at race time and make a pass."

By then they had dropped to fourth fastest in the field, behind Twig Zeigler, Pat Foster, and Dale Pulde. Prudhomme made a single run at 1 P.M. and went 6.352, the fastest qualifying time and also an official NHRA record for funny cars, the first in Don Prudhomme's career. "We just put the car back on the trailer," said Weasel, "and went back to the motel."

Tom McEwen, Prudhomme's rival and teammate, ranked sixteenth on Saturday but early Sunday got bumped from the field. He made several extra attempts but failed to qualify.

Another drag racing veteran suffering problems was Don Garlits. Garlits had won the top fuel title at Tulsa the previous weekend, but at Indianapolis couldn't find the proper combination. He failed again and again to qualify until finally, late on Sunday, time remained for only one more run. Spectators jammed the stands to see Garlits face his moment of truth, and as Garlits moved to the line, they rose in expectation.

With a roar he shot down the track, and when the spectators saw the time of 6.26 flash on the sign next to Garlits' lane, they cheered in relief, knowing they would get to see him race the following day. Garlits' time then qualified him sixteenth, which under the standard NHRA pairings would have allowed him to meet the slowest qualifier in the thirty-two man top fuel field. Garlits' crew drove their truck to pick up their driver, waving casually to the crowd as though there had been no worry, it was all by plan.

The following day they were less happy. Faster runs by two other drivers had dropped Garlits farther down on the qualifying list, and instead of the slowest qualifier, he met Gary Beck, the defending champion from Edmonton, Canada. Beck eliminated Garlits in the first round and went on to win his second title in two years. The following weekend at a meet at Suffolk Raceway, however, Garlits ran a 5.97. Thus do the fortunes of drag racers rise and fall.

But the fortunes of Don Prudhomme seemed to be rising at Indianapolis. As early as five-thirty Monday morning, his crew arrived at the track to lay out all their tools and extra parts so that in case of sudden need they wouldn't have to search for them. They even fitted rings to spare pistons, a precaution that might save them several minutes in between-round repairs.

At six Prudhomme got out of bed. As is his custom the day of a race, he didn't have breakfast. He did drink a Coke. He climbed into a rental car to drive to the track alone, another of his customs. "I thought about the race going out," he later remembered. "I was in a pretty good mood. I was relaxed and felt very confident."

In the first round Tom Prock of Detroit ran 6.30 seconds but had the bad luck to do it behind Don Prudhomme, who ran 6.27. "That was some run we laid down," Snake would recall, "but let me tell you, that was some run they laid down too. Prock ran the third fastest e.t. in the meet. And got beat. He easily could have knocked me right out of the show."

McCulloch met Billy Meyer of Waco, Texas, in the first round and beat him 6.40 to 6.49. Snake beat Richard Tharp in the second round (6.39 to 6.51) but came close to being disqualified. Prudhomme's car, right after the start, had veered toward the center line. He touched the line and appeared to have crossed it, which would have resulted in disqualification. Then he straightened the car out and continued down the track. The winner's light lit next to Prudhomme's lane. Weasel and Jerry turned toward starter Buster Couch, who told them, "He's out!"

They drove down to the end of the track to tell Prudhomme the bad news. As soon as he saw their faces, he knew something was wrong, but when he learned what, he decided to protest. "I was ready to fight somebody," he admitted. Snake planned, if necessary, to force the officials to halt the meet and walk with him out on the track and point out the tire marks where he had crossed the line. If necessary, he would have dodged speeding cars to look at the marks himself. Buster Couch undoubtedly realized this, because when he saw Snake approaching, coiled and ready to strike, he simply waved for him to go up to the starting tower. Snake climbed the stairs to where the top NHRA officials sat in judgment to determine his future. When he descended from the tower, he gave a quick "thumbs up" sign and rushed to his pits to get ready for the next round. The judges had informed him that they had watched through binoculars, and he had only touched the line, not crossed it.

"The car was vibrating going down the course," Prudhomme would explain later. "It was shaking, and it whipped me toward the other lane. A lot of things happen. See, that's the real shame about a drag race. I'll tell you. I was at a press conference the other day, and one of the writers asked, he says, 'It doesn't look to me like you do too much. It doesn't take much to drive one of those things. Just stab the throttle and go in a straight line.'

"Well, I'd like to have one of those guys ride the car. I mean, it's an experience. I'm not trying to say that my car is harder to drive at 200 mph than an Indianapolis car—but it's hard. *I* think it's hard. If I thought it was easy, I'd tell you it's easy. But a lot of things can happen in six seconds. That six seconds sometimes feels like a lifetime, especially when you look out the side and there's a car right next to you.

"There are so many things that can happen. Tire vibrations. The car gets out of shape. While that car is out of shape and while the tires are shaking, not only are you concerned about beating the guy next to you, especially in a big race like Indy, but you're thinking: *I've got to fix that before the next round.* There must be a million thoughts that go through your mind during the six-second run. Then people look at me at the end of the day and say, 'Boy, you sure look tired.' Doggone right. I have thought about every thought in the world."

Prudhomme once was asked if there was any particular talent, or skill, or natural ability that made him such a good driver. "I can't really say," he responded. "I don't call myself a better driver than Ed McCulloch, Jim Nicoll, Tom McEwen. Any of those guys can beat you at any given time. And if they beat me, I sure don't think they're better drivers than I am. Not at all. It gets back to that short little six-second run. It gets back to the point of knowing your machinery. Now you can take a new driver, a green kid, and put him in my car. He goes to the starting line, hits the throttle, and that baby sits low e.t. of the meet. Perhaps he could win the race that day. But where it really counts is when you take that car from *that* track and to *another* track and get the car dialed in to run fast. That's where it all comes in. What does that car do when it leaves the starting line? Like when I go out and do my burnouts. Just like yesterday—"

The "yesterday" Snake referred to was an AHRA race at Orange County International Raceway. He continued: "Yesterday I knew doing my burnouts that I was going to smoke the tires. There was no possible way to avoid it, because we had hurried between rounds and put a new engine in the car. I did my burnout. Hit the throttle and lit the tires to get them hot. The car had too much power. So I backed up, hit it behind the starting line, and did several dry burnouts. *Crack!* The engine really grabbed. *Oh, my god,* I thought. *I'm in trouble.* So when the light came on, I tried to move out easily, but there was nothing I could do. She just went up in smoke. It was all over. I was history. But at Indy the track was good. The car was running good. I knew I was running good. I would have raced King Kong if he was sitting in the next lane to me."

But Don Prudhomme's rival in the finals at Indianapolis would be not King Kong, but Ed McCulloch. Prudhomme stalked around his car, staring at it as though trying to recall any tasks that might have been forgotten. He lay a hand on the front wheel. "Hey, don't we need to look at this?"

"That's all taken care of," Weasel told him.

Prudhomme bent over the supercharger to assure himself that its drive belt was tight, and a drop of sweat fell from his nose. He raised his left arm, wiped his face on his T-shirt, and walked over to his trailer to check the temperature and humidity gauges. The humidity had been high all day but had fallen slightly since the previous run. If it continued to drop, he would make a slight jet change just before climbing into the car for the final round.

Prudhomme sat down in the doorway of his trailer, relaxed for two seconds, then stood up to talk to Ed Pink. It was now 5:01 P.M. On the racetrack, Hell on Wheels, a drag car built to look like a tank, was making an exhibition run to keep the crowd amused while the finalists prepared their cars. At that moment Ed McCulloch's car was towed past toward the staging lane. Don Prudhomme glanced at it, went to his truck to get another cold drink, wiped his hands on a rag, and waited as the last bolt was tightened in place. "Okay, let's go race," he said.

8

"HE LOOKS AT YOU, AND YOU LOOK AT HIM"

As he was being towed toward the staging area, Don Prudhomme squinted in the bright sunlight and thought: *Well, we either win or we're runner-up.* The preparations were over. The engine had been tuned. The clutch had been adjusted. The fuel had been mixed and poured into the tank. All the mechanical tasks related to the automobile had been completed, and there remained only the physical act of driving it down the racetrack as fast as it would go.

He thought now for the first time about the money. The weekend before, he had won $25,000 at Tulsa, and the posted price for this race was $15,950 for the winner, $4,650 for runner-up. Of course, some of this sum was in so-called contingency awards: money posted by sponsors such as Goodyear, Wynn's, or Mr. Gasket. You collected only if you had signed an advertising contract with the sponsors and had their name on the side of your car. The maximum sum Snake could hope to collect was around $15,000. "I never thought about losing the race," he said later. "But runner-up isn't the worst thing in the world that can happen to you. It's better than going out the first round."

Weasel stopped the truck next to the fence at the far edge of the racetrack. Ahead of it in line waited a single funny car, that of Ed McCulloch. Two lanes away sat two more racing machines: the cars of pro stock finalists Bob Glidden and Wayne Gapp. The pits for fuel dragsters and various modified cars were on the other, eastern side of the track. In another staging area top fuel finalists Gary Beck and Carl Olson waited with their crews.

Only a day before, the scene in the staging lanes looked like a freeway traffic jam. Cars waited door to door, bumper to bumper, the crush spilling backward even onto the access road. Drivers, crewmen, spectators, photographers moved between the cars. But now, in the last hour of a long weekend, the staging lanes were mostly empty pavement. Some drops of oil. Puddles of water from the radiators of those who had passed before. It had come down, in each of the three remaining professional classes, to one man against one man.

There were no last-minute adjustments, no sense of panic, among these last few competitors—only quiet waiting. Overhead a helicopter trailed a banner promoting "Honest Charley's Speed Shops." But nobody looked up to see it.

Prudhomme climbed out of his race car still clad in fire pants, boots, and his multipatterned Snake T-shirt. It seemed remarkably clean considering the amount of work he had performed on his car. He walked over to his truck and found a blue Cragar cap, which he placed on his head as protection against the sun. McCulloch rose from where he was sitting on the front wheel of his car and walked over to talk to Snake. He wore a cap that said "Ed Pink Racing Engines." His T-shirt seemed smudged with the grime from a hundred engines.

"What do you think?" asked Ed McCulloch.

To a drag racer the question "What do you think?" has a single meaning. It means: What do you think about splitting the money? It means: No matter who wins, the purse will be divided in equal shares. It means: Before the drivers hit the switch to start their engines, they are guaranteed equal money.

Many reasons exist why finalists in a drag race might consider such a split. The main reason is that so many problems can occur to defeat them between staging lane and starting line that have nothing to do with their ability to drive fast. They can start the car for the final round and not have any oil pressure. They can start the car, do a burnout, and blow a rod. They might not even start. They might hit the switch and find the battery dead. They could lose the coin flip and have to race in a lane so slick with oil that they wouldn't be able to outdrag even a J-stocker. "There are so many things that can happen," Snake admitted later. "I've had *so* many disappointments. I'll tell you. Like especially last year. You hate even to start thinking about what can happen." There was a touch of pathos in Snake's voice as he spoke.

Afterward Don Prudhomme would not be certain that Ed McCulloch was serious when he said, "What do you think?" or whether he merely was probing, searching for some sign of weakness on Snake's part. If so, Snake gave no such sign. "There isn't that much money up to split," he replied.

"Yeah, you're right."

Prudhomme fixed McCulloch with a quizzical look. "You're not mad?"

"No, okay."

Prudhomme smiled. "Then why did you even ask?"

The two drivers laughed, and for a moment there was a break in the tension that had been building for the last hour, for the entire afternoon, for the past six days. But this moment passed quickly. The smiles froze, then faded. Prudhomme reached into the pocket of his fire suit for a twenty-five-cent piece. McCulloch looked fearfully at the coin resting lightly between the forefinger and thumb of Snake's right hand, because he knew that despite all their preparations, despite the competence of their mechanics, despite the superiority of one car over another, national championships often are decided by the simple act of flipping a coin to decide lanes. It is almost as though fate sits back and watches drag racers go through all their motions, then—at the last minute—intervenes.

"Most guys are nervous wrecks when it comes time to flip the coin," Prudhomme later confessed. "It's not just a six-second run, you know. It seems like six hours building up to run six seconds. It starts back in the pits and works its way to where you are towing the car to the staging lane, until finally you pull in beside the guy you are going to race. And he looks at you. And you look at him. And his crew guys are looking at your race car to see if there is any oil dripping off it from the run before. And your crew is looking at their exhaust pipes to see if they burned a piston the round before, because when that happens you often get aluminum spray on the pipes. You size each other up. Finally the big moment comes when that guy walks up to you and says, 'Flip you for lanes.' You almost faint."

Snake flipped the coin.

"Call it," he said.

"Heads," called McCulloch.

The year before, Ed McCulloch had won three major meets in a row before going to Englishtown, New Jersey, for the Summernationals. He made the finals against Don Schumacher, thus had a strong shot at a fourth straight win in a major NHRA meet, almost an unprecedented feat—but it was a one-lane racetrack. Oil from a blown engine had made one of the lanes overly slick. McCulloch lost the flip, smoked the ties, and lost the race.

"Invariably when we go to these tracks, there is a better lane," Prudhomme explains. "The right lane is better than the left, or the left better than the right. I know that sounds ridiculous when the pavement is supposed to be the same, but someone will break an engine in one of the lanes. They clean it up the best they can, but the asphalt absorbs some of the oil. They can't get it out. You can't see it, but when you run there, the tires will slip. Or it may rain, and one lane will retain the dampness more than the other. Dirt from the return road blows across the track. There are so many variables. If you come up to the line behind someone and they break a motor, boy, the race is history. I don't care how good you've been running."

In AHRA championship meets, however, lane choice goes to the driver with the fastest previous round. A driver concerned with lane choice will race full speed even if an opponent breaks on the line, assuring him an easy solo victory. This provides a better show for the fans, but it also provides some security for those drivers who run consistently fast. The previous year at an NHRA meet in Amarillo, Texas, drivers voted whether to abandon the coin flip in favor of lane selection by fastest e.t. Both Prudhomme and McCulloch favored this idea. Many lesser drivers did not, apparently figuring they had a better chance of victory trusting luck rather than skill.

The track at Indianapolis normally provides excellent traction. Most racers consider it the best in the world. It is safe; it is fast. One reason for its being fast is the large number of fast cars that race there. Good traction depends in part on pavement, but also on the rubber laid down *on* the pavement. Cars that take longer than ten seconds to drive a quarter mile do not lay down much rubber, particularly at half track. Dragsters and funny cars, however, spin their tires all the way through the lights.

For this particular race, the track at IRP was definitely a two-lane track, despite pro stock driver Larry Huff's having broken an engine, oiling the left lane early that morning. After the oil had been cleaned up, Prudhomme had run his 6.27 e.t. (fastest of the meet) in that same lane. He made his next two passes, both of them slower, including the one in which he smoked his tires, in the right lane. McCulloch won his first-found coin flip and, partly because in two previous years at IRP (including tire testing) he had only run the left lane once, chose the right. Afterward he lost the flip and had to run on the left. It didn't seem to affect his times.

The coin landed tails.

"I'm probably going to take the right lane," said Snake, "but I want to go look at it first."

They borrowed motorcycles from two NHRA officials and drove to the starting line. The two rivals stood staring at the track, which was black from the rubber laid on top of it. Snake bent and pressed his palm to the pavement of the right lane. If you walk on a drag track, it pulls at the bottom of your shoes as though you were treading on molasses. The track, as Snake felt it, had this tacky feeling. "Yeah, I'm going to take the right lane," he said. Then he added cautiously, "As long as nothing happens before we run."

McCulloch thus was forced to accept the left lane, but he was satisfied. The lanes seemed about equal, and he was pleased not to have to make a choice. In fact, he thought he might even have the slightly better lane. "The right lane was starting to ball up a bit, and the left lane was clean," he said later. Prudhomme, too, thought the left lane might have been slightly better. When the rubber on a racetrack rolls up in balls, driving on it is like driving over BBs. But Snake believed any difference to be slight, and he thought he would feel more comfortable in the lane he had used the two previous rounds. Whichever lane was better, it would not be a factor in determining victory that day.

The two mounted the motorcycles and returned to the staging area. McCulloch's mechanic asked him, "Same plan?"

McCulloch nodded his head. He shrugged. He walked to the back of his truck and found a plastic cup containing mostly ice. He drank.

9

"PEOPLE GO CRAZY
IN THESE CARS"

Don Prudhomme also now had a plastic cup in his hand. He popped the last ice cube from it into his mouth and began to chew. He sat on the frame of his race car, head down. He began to pick at dirt underneath his fingernails. Some years before, whenever he got nervous, Snake would twist a finger in the tight rings of his curly hair. His wife, Lynn, eventually broke him of that habit. So now he picked dirt out of his fingernails.

He suddenly looked up. "Hey, that fire bottle."

"Right," said Weasel.

"Yeah, check it now."

Because of the extreme danger of fire, Snake's Cuda carried four seven-and-a-half-pound fire extinguishers aboard. Two were attached to the frame, trained at the engine. Two nestled next to the driver's shoulders, trained on him. After the second round, one of the fire bottles had been bumped and discharged accidentally. In the rush of preparing the car for the semifinals and finals, the empty fire bottle had not been replaced.

Prudhomme remembered to check the fire bottle because he thought of the piston that had been slightly burned the precious round. He thought the engine probably would remain together long enough for him to run the race—otherwise, he would have changed pistons instead of adjusting the clutch—but he also knew the threat of fire was higher than usual. "That's something, isn't it?" he admitted later. "Before I even go down the track, I'm thinking I'll probably have a fire. People go crazy in these cars sometimes to win a race, you know that? I mean, they will just blow the body off it. Blow an engine right out of the chassis. Sometimes you get so involved in winning that you would drive the car down through there naked."

Of course, NHRA has rules that make naked driving illegal. Drivers must wear fire suits, boots, gloves, and face masks that meet strict standards. Their clothing must be able to resist 1,850 degrees of heat for a minimum of ten seconds. Each funny car must carry onboard fire extinguishers containing a minimum of twenty pounds of Freon, or FE-1301. Prudhomme had thirty pounds in his car, so even with one bottle discharged, he would have been operating within the rules.

But you still can get killed operating within the rules even though the souvenir program for the U.S. Nationals boasted that there had been no deaths in the professional categories at NHRA sanctioned drag races "for several years now." (The last death had been John Mulligan in 1969.) Also according to the program, the injury rate to contestants competing in NHRA-sanctioned events was nearly fifteen times lower than the national motor vehicle highway rate.

There are several reasons for this. You don't find drunks on drag strips. You don't have crowded traffic conditions. There are no narrow roads, unlit stretches, or poorly marked turns at a drag strip. People don't use their cars to commit suicide, as often occurs in the case of one-car accidents on public roads.

But regardless of what NHRA statistics imply, those drivers who push their cars into the six-second bracket very definitely are in a high-risk business. "We're constantly trying to upgrade our safety regulations," admits Wally Parks, NHRA president, "but almost every rule is based on a mishap. A change in speed or conditions can cause new hazards, and someone may get killed before we realize it."

The rules are necessary because of the desire of drivers and owners for victory. "The cars will run hard and fast if you put them in a destruct position," explains Pat Minnick, owner of Chitown Hustler. "In other words, you can set up the engine to run 1,200 feet and blow up. You'll run fast, but the race is 1,320 feet long, and new engines cost money. If you set up the engine to destruct at 1,400 feet, you won't go quickest and fastest, but you'll have a margin of safety. You can shut off at 1,320 feet and save the engine. Where it gets tricky is setting that engine up to *exactly* 1,320 feet."

Thus in their constant quest for speed, funny car drivers may be compared to bullfighters. They stand in the center of the arena waving their red cloaks in the face of the bull, goading him to action. The bull paws the ground. He snorts. He charges. His horns pass near the leg of the matador. The crowd shouts, "Olé!" The matador waves his cloak again. The bull turns, sees his enemy, and, head down, charges again, his horn brushing the matador's leg. The crowd shouts, "Olé!" Again the red cloak waves, the bull charges; only this time his horn sinks into the matador's belly, and with a twitch of his neck the powerful animal flicks the matador over his back. The crowd no longer cheers.

On Sunday, while the unqualified drivers were trying to push their cars harder and faster to make the sixteen-man final field, the horns of the bull brushed one matador's leg. Mike Mitchell (who bills himself as the "World's Fastest Hippie") made an attempt to qualify. Suddenly his car burst into flames, and he rocketed down the track, a burning comet. Fire trucks quickly reached the race car. The fires were doused. The car escaped with minor damage. The driver emerged unhurt. Too bad for Mitchell's chances to qualify, but that's racing.

Several weeks later in Irvine, California, the bull's horn grazed Don Prudhomme. Snake was running in an AHRA event and had already survived the first round on Saturday night But he disliked the way his car was running. For some reason that nobody seems to understand, the track at Orange County International Raceway is very difficult to drive fast on. Despite having been repaved often, the asphalt seems to impart some sort of vibration to the fast cars, shaking them severely, causing them often to fall apart. Prudhomme came out to the track early on Sunday morning to make more practice runs before the afternoon finals. "I was trying to lay a 6.30 run down on a 6.60 track," he would admit.

Don was towed to the starting line by his truck. Don's wife, Lynn, sat in the back seat of the truck. Don's cousin, Mark Prudhomme, was driving. Snake's crew went through their last ritual of preparation, firing the car, pouring water for the burnouts, guiding him to the right spot in the lane. Then Mark moved the truck to a point ahead of the starting line and parked just outside the guardrail, not more than ten feet from where Prudhomme would pass.

The last staging light lit. The sound of Snake's engine changed from a crackle to a low roar as he fed more fuel, raising the revolutions, getting ready to charge the moment the light turned green. It did and:

RRRRAAAAAAAAAAA!!!

His car rushed past, a blur of yellow, then suddenly *red!* "Oh, my God! Oh my God!" cried Lynn. Not fifty feet off the line, the car had caught fire. Flames roared up from beneath the headers to lick at the Cuda's side. There was a wall of fire near the open window where Snake sat, braking, fighting the steering wheel, trying to keep the car pointed straight down the track even though he no longer could see.

Mark, who had been standing near the front fender of the idling truck, reared instantly and jumped back into the drivers' seat, his face drawn, worry in his eyes. "Quick, Mark, quick!" Lynn pleaded. Mark slammed the truck into gear and took off down the road, chasing the race car which had careened dizzily down the track, flames still licking its sides.

"Hurry, Mark!" Lynn urged. "The extinguishers didn't stop the fire!" Ahead, a fire truck and an ambulance had already begun to converge on the spot where Snake's car finally had halted. Mark braked the truck quickly.

But Lynn was wrong. The on-board extinguishers had worked, and the fire was out. Snake came rolling out the right side window. He rolled, not climbed out, or even fell, the way a tumbler might roll onto a mat, the response of a well-conditioned athlete. He bounced up to start walking around the back of his car in circles, as though dazed. At first it appeared that he might suddenly collapse, but when he removed his helmet, the angry look on his face indicated he wasn't hurt.

Lynn was at his side, talking quietly to her husband, and he handed her his helmet and gloves. His fire suit had been singed. The decorative stripes on his arm had been burned off. The matador, after he emerges from the arena, often has blood on his uniform. It is the bull's blood, not his. Usually. Prudhomme had only been brushed by the horns.

The damage to his car was more severe, two gaping holes having been blown through the engine block. Almost instantly Snake was off striding toward the pits, barking instructions over his shoulder to Weasel and Jerry, who, having been abandoned by the truck, had run half the length of the drag strip to reach him. "Get that car back fast," Snake snapped. "We've got to change that engine!"

One of the meet officials approached Lynn. "Let us know if he suffered any burns," he said, as though Prudhomme, like a child, could not be trusted to care for himself.

"He's all right," said Lynn. "He's all right."

An hour later Snake was back at the starting line with a new engine bolted into his now-tarnished racing machine. He had to face another team with a much slower car. He should have been able to defeat them easily. The car's owner kept apologizing to Snake for not being able to offer him competition. But the new engine proved too much power, and Snake smoked the tires. He lost and went home early that day.

When asked how often a fire happens, Snake admits, "Quite often." "The worst fire I ever had was up in Seattle about a year ago with my old funny car. The run before, I had gone 222 mph, which was pretty fast at the time, a track record by about 10 mph. But I had hurt a piston, and we didn't have time to change it," he said.

"I was whistling down through there ahead of the guy I was racing. Just as I was ready to click it off coming into the lights, the car caught fire. The fire was so bad that it actually ate up all the oxygen underneath. A racing car going that fast creates a vacuum below. That helps hold the car to the ground. The air flowing over the roof also keeps the car stable. In this case the fire disrupted the air going both under and over the car, so I flew at the other end.

"The car actually popped up on its rear wheels. Then the wind got under the body, it blew it a hundred feet into the air. That allowed the car to bounce back down on all four wheels. It hit so hard it knocked me out for a minute. The fire burned the devil out of me. Ruined my fire suit. I had bruises on my arms too, but they're gone now.

"When you have a fire, you have to get on the brakes quick. But there's usually oil under the tires, and the car slides around. You've got to get her stopped as fast as you can and try to keep your cool without slamming into the guardrail. It's hard to get to all the controls, no matter where they are, because the heat is so great. Your goggles fog right over, so you can't see anything. Can't even tell if the car is still on fire or not when you stop. You don't know for sure, so you just get out as fast as you possibly can. Or if you can't get out, hope that somebody gets down there in time to get you out. But it's hard for people to get to you because of the heat.

"Now that fire I had yesterday was a little fire. That was nothing compared to some of them. I've seen guys get out of some fires who have just barely survived. I'm pretty careful. I try to watch it as best I can. But you're there to win. Thinking about it now, I probably wouldn't do it, but at Indianapolis I would have burned that car to the ground in order to beat McCulloch."

Many members of the general public believe auto racing fans attend events such as Daytona, Watkins Glen, and Indianapolis to watch drivers get killed. That's not true. First of all, auto racing fans (like fans in any sport) worship their athlete heroes. People who Don

Prudhomme has never met, will never meet, think of him as some kind of god, just as Snake himself once considered Chris Karamesines a god. People do not enjoy losing their heroes or gods.

Fans sometimes enjoy seeing spectacular accidents, the screech of tires, the clash of metal, the clouds of smoke. But those who enjoy that type of spectacle are best off attending demolition derbies, where wrecks are guaranteed. Anybody who has attended many auto races, whether on oval tracks or drag strips, soon realizes that what follows any spectacular crash is a long, dull wait while trucks tow away the automobiles and workers clean debris from the track.

But perhaps the best argument is offered by Jim McKay, the ABC sports commentator: "After a spectacular crash the fans want to see the driver climb out of the car and wave to the crowd to prove that he isn't hurt, because auto racing is a sport that pits man against the machine. If he fails to climb out, if he is killed, then it means that the machine has won."

Waiting to race the machine of Ed McCulloch, ten minutes before they would go to the line, Don Prudhomme had already dismissed the thought of accident from his mind even while Jerry was fastening the new fire bottle in place. Snake sat on the frame of his car, one arm holding onto the pole that supported its fiberglass body. He wiped his forehead with a rag. He looked around him. "Everything checked?" he asked. Weasel nodded his head. Snake stood up. He kicked a paper cup that was lying on the ground. He wiped his forehead once again. He sat back down.

He was thinking about the start and whether the adjustments he had made would solve his problems of having smoked the tires in the last round. He was pretty sure that they would because he had adjusted the clutch. It would transmit the power from the engine to the rear wheels more gradually, but the looser clutch could cause another problem.

There are two photoelectric light beams eight inches apart at ground level in each lane on the starting line. When the driver eases his car up to the line and breaks the first beam, he is prestaged. An amber light flashes on top of the Christmas tree, the pole that signals the drivers when to leave. (The starting pole received its name because with red, yellow, and green lights it does resemble a Christmas tree.)

Once the driver is prestaged, he continues to creep forward, being guided by the starter. When he moves his front wheels eight inches farther forward, they break the second beam of lights and he is staged. A second amber light flashes near his lane on the Christmas tree. (A drag racer describing this would say he "put out his second light," even though in effect he would be putting the light on.) When both drivers have moved into position (i.e., put out their lights), the starter presses a button in his hand, which begins the automatic countdown.

At small races with amateur drivers, there often are a series of amber (or yellow) warning lights at intervals of one-fifth of a second before the green light flashes go. It is:

Yellow-yellow-yellow-yellow-yellow
GREEN!

Professional drivers get a single warning light before receiving the signal to go. This is called a pro start, and it is:

Yellow

GREEN!

Most experienced drivers hit the throttle even before they see green, because it takes a fraction of a second for them to react to the light and another fraction for the car to react to them. If they wait to see the green, they're history. But if they try to outguess the light and move too quickly, they risk red-lighting. A red light flashes in their lane if they leave before the green. They are disqualified. Again, they're history.

The top drivers also nail their cars—that is, as soon as both cars are staged, they gently press the throttle, revving the engine, raising its revolutions, pushing it up from 1,500 rpm to maybe 3,000 rpm, keeping their foot on the brake so the engine won't drag them across the line. The engine, prerevved, will reach full power quicker once they move. But for Don Prudhomme this would offer too much risk. He had adjusted his clutch, tightening it. If he tried to nail his car, even with his foot on the brake, the engine might pull him forward, breaking the beam and causing him to red-light. So Snake decided that rather than nail the car, he would drive it off the line—that is, let the engine idle and hit the throttle only at the moment he wanted to go. This would mean McCulloch probably would beat him off the line. It would mean Prudhomme would have to drive past McCulloch at the other end of the track to win. It would mean a very exiting race.

10

"YOU'VE GOT TO GET MEAN"

The loudspeaker crackled in the staging area: "Station Able. Get ready to start moving those funny cars out here now."

Don Prudhomme rose from his seat once more and walked to his truck. He opened the rear door. He grabbed his fire jacket off the seat and shrugged it onto his shoulders. He zipped it up, pressing the collar tight around his neck.

Weasel placed Don's helmet with his gloves, face stocking, and goggles next to the strut supporting the steering wheel. Snake climbed into the car. McCulloch jumped from the tailgate of his truck and climbed into his car. Snake fumbled through the gear in the helmet until he found a thin, skintight pair of gloves like those a golfer might wear. He pulled them over his hands. Next, he reached for the face stocking, a light tan hood made of fireproof Nomex. When he pulled it on over his head, only his eyes and nose peeked through the circular hole.

Next, he donned his gas mask, blue, with a nose like a pig's snout and a side filter to prevent fumes and smoke from reaching his lungs. Then his helmet, open-faced, similar to those worn by motorcyclists and with the name "Snake" painted across the front.

Now Snake stuck out his hands. It was like the gesture you would expect from a surgeon as he prepared to operate on a patient. Weasel placed heavy fireproof gloves on Snake's outstretched hands and tugged them tightly in place. Snake reached up with his now-thick fingers and pulled his goggles down over his eyes. "Start moving the funny cars up to the pad," said the loudspeaker. Snake placed his hands on the steering wheel of his car. It was not like the wheel of your regular car, but more like a pair of handles attached to a long rod.

The truck moved forward towing the race car behind. They drove only a short distance to the so-called launch pad, on line with the two lanes on which they would run, but roughly 150 yards behind the starting area. They were ready to run. Then an NHRA official came over and told them they planned to run the pro stocks first.

As pro stockers Bob Glidden and Wayne Gapp fired their cars and moved to the starting line, Prudhomme climbed out of his driving seat and carefully removed all the equipment he had just put on. He said to Weasel, "Go tell McCulloch I'm out of the car in case he wants to relax too."

Snake moved to his truck and wiped his forehead with a towel. He stared over to where Ed McCulloch was now climbing out of his car. He wanted to beat him badly. McCulloch, whose garage was only two doors from his garage back in California, whom he sometimes eats lunch with, whom he sometimes cycles with on the trails above Granada Hills, whose ability he respects, some of whose sponsors he also shares, and he still wanted to beat him. He wanted to make him eat his dust. He wanted to put him on the truck, make him history. He wanted to defeat him in front of those 60,000 fans in the stands and the hundreds of thousands of others who would read about the race in *National Dragster, Hot Rod, Drag News,* and in the record books for the next hundred years or more.

A few months earlier they had met in the finals of a race in Rockford, Illinois. "I ran quicker than he did, and he still beat me," Snake recalled. "I was very unhappy about that. *Very* unhappy. So at Indianapolis, when qualifying was almost over and it looked as though we might meet in the first round, he said to me, 'Well, Snake, no problem. I'll just leave on you and beat you.' He really burned me when he said that. I didn't let him know it, though. So I said, 'No problem, Ed. Just leave whenever you want. Probably about the three-quarters point, I'll just drive on around you.' His guys went: Urrrrghhhhh! Everybody got mad when I said that. I said, 'See you later, fellows.' I was cocky about it. I knew I was being cocky. But I couldn't let him get up on me."

"Does much needling go on between drivers?" Snake was asked.

"Constantly," he replied slowly, as though to emphasize the word. "Constantly. It's really a battle. Oh, yeah.

You always try and psych the other guy out and pull anything you can pull. It just constantly goes on."

"Can you actually be close friends with these people?"

"It's hard to be. I try to go to the races a lot of times with the attitude of hating everybody. I go there disliking guys. I go there not talking to the other racers, kind of sticking to myself. You've got to build yourself up if you want to win. And I'm a bad loser, too. I always say, a good loser is a loser. And that attitude helps.

"Now when I went to Indy, McEwen and I were in a battle. We're partners, but we had some personal problems going into the race. And I went there in a bad mood. I didn't want to be fooled with. Gee, I think that really helped me. I just wanted to beat everybody. Guys who go there happy-go-lucky, once in a while you see them in the winning circle, but not too often. You've got to get mean."

Yet before the previous rounds Snake often could be found sitting in a circle of drivers, maybe not talking with them, but at least sitting. When he had climbed out of his car to cool off, he courteously had sent Weasel over to tell McCulloch what he was doing in case the other driver wanted to do the same.

"Well, you've got to be friends," Snake admits. "I mean, a guy will come up and talk to you. I go up and talk to them. We all talk. But as far as I'm concerned, they are the enemy. And they are there to beat me.

"They'll try anything. They will drive right over the top of you to beat you. Like Richard Tharp went up there to race Pat Foster in the first round. Pat drives the Barry

Setzer car. Well, Tharp and Foster are the best of friends. I always see them running around together.

"Tharp hadn't been running as good as Foster. He was driving a different car. His Blue Max had burned down the month before. So all they had to do is leave the starting line at the same time, and I would have bet you a hundred-dollar bill that Foster would smoke him off. So when they got to the starting line, what does Tharp do? Foster has both his staging lights lit, and Tharp creeps up there real, real slow. He hasn't staged yet. It breaks your train of thought. You are thinking about the lights, yet you know the other guy hasn't staged yet. You're thinking: *What is he doing over there? How come he's not staged?* You don't want to take your eyes off the tree for fear they'll start the countdown. *Click!* They'll turn the light on, and you've lost the race. But how come he's not staged? And this is all in that six-second run, right?

"Tharp put out his first staging light, pushes his clutch in, and hits his throttle. *Rap! Rap!* And that goofed Pat up some more. Tharp finally put out his last staging light, hit the throttle again, and Pat left. He was so goofed up from Tharp doing all of this monkey motion stuff that it just psyched him out. He left too soon. Red-lighted. Tharp didn't care. He had won his round. Heck, he was running on seven cylinders at the time. No way he could have won the race. They don't say, 'Well, fellows, let's come back and do that over again.' You are out of the race. You go home."

Prudhomme was asked if Tharp, whom he had raced in the second round, had played any games with him.

"Yeah, he did. He sure did! I don't know if you noticed that run, but he takes a long time backing up. Most guys just zoom back after their burnout. I told my guys when we go to race him, just take it easy. Let him fire first. We are going to cool it. So Tharp fired. We fired. And we both went to the bleach box. I let Tharp go ahead and do his burnout. I sat there a minute, and I did mine. Then I waited down the track for a few seconds to get everything straightened out, got it in reverse, and started backing up. Tharp had already gone out of my eyesight. But as I was backing up, I passed him. He was chugging back: Whuppp. Whuppp. Whuppp. *Whuppp-whuppp-whuppp.* I said, 'Boy, he's fooling with me.' So I backed up and waited behind the staging light. He had backed up by now and was ready to go forward. I went forward. Just cleaned my tires—chirped the tires, we call it. Hit the throttle: *Rupp! Ruppp!* Made sure everything was hooked up. He's still jacking around back there, and I knew he was playing with me. I watched him and decided I didn't care what, I wasn't going until I saw the green. He got out on me. He pushed me. I had to drive around him."

"Now Leroy was no games. He just went heads-up. But they try all this stuff on me. Like I say, they are your enemy. I mean, your friend wouldn't do that to you, right? He's your pal. You run around with him. He wouldn't do that to you. But they do."

A voice crackled over the loudspeaker: "Get ready to light the funnies." It was now 5:18 P.M.

Snake went through the ritual of dress again. He became the knight climbing into his armor, about to mount his horse, readying himself for the joust. He became the matador donning his spangled costume, folding his cloak over his arm, sheathing his sword, ready to fight the bull. But mostly he became brother to the classic western gunslinger, who straightens his neckerchief, tugs at his gun belt, adjusts his holster, pats his Stetson hat in place, then saunters out onto the dusty Main Street of Dodge City, Laramie, Cheyenne, to meet his opponent. It is high noon. The townspeople peer out from their windows. The first one to draw and shoot straight wins, and the bad guy lies dead in the dust. *Bam!* Fastest gun in the West!

Sitting in the seat of his funny car now, Snake waited patiently as Weasel fastened the safety belt and shoulder harness that might save his life in case of a crash. The bucket seat cradling his body and the double roll bar over his head offered him enough protection so that, in theory, he would be safer crashing in his racer at 230 mph than he would be in an accident in his Continental Mark IV at one-third that speed on the Los Angeles Freeway. *In theory.* "I'm more frightened driving to and from the track than I am driving at the track," claims Snake, and you want to believe him. But it takes courage to climb into a 2,000-horsepower car and literally be fired out of a gun. Drag racers, however, never think long about the dangers; otherwise they would cease to be drag racers. "What does it feel like sitting on the starting line in a fuel racer?" Don Schumacher once was asked. "That you could do anything you wanted to, including walk on water," he replied.

Weasel finished buckling Snake's safety harness, and Jerry taped the sides of the belt as an added protection against fire. Then both crewmen removed the safety pins from the fire extinguishers, Jerry the two up front, Weasel the two in the cockpit. They showed Snake the pins, so he knew they were out. It has not escaped the attention of Don Prudhomme that those safety pins resemble the pins you pull from a grenade before throwing it. "We sit there ready to explode off the line," he says.

Weasel checked the parachute pack in the rear and signaled Snake that it was secure. (At a race in Bristol, Tennessee, two weeks later, Pat Foster was disqualified when his parachute came loose during a burnout.) The truck had been moved into position for starting, and the battery-run aircraft starter lay ready on the ground. Jerry handed Weasel a bottle of gasoline for priming the engine. Snake checked his mag switch to make sure it was off. If they turned the engine over with the switch on, there might be fuel still in the supercharger, which could ignite and cause a small explosion. Snake adjusted his goggles.

"Light 'em, Bob," came a voice over the loudspeaker. "Light the funnies." The time was 5:21 P.M.

Weasel signaled McCulloch's crew to make certain they were ready. There would be no games, just hard, heads-up racing.

11

"RUN CAR, JUST RUN"

There was a splash of unburned fuel from the header pipes as Snake's Cuda shouted its readiness to race. Smoke filled the air. Noise filled the air.

Jerry lifted the starting motor into the back of the truck. He removed the support poles holding the fiberglass body up and threw them also in the back of the truck, then fastened the tailgate. The truck started up toward the starting line. Jerry lowered the body, snapped it in place, tested it to see it was secure, then started running toward the line.

Don Prudhomme, now barely visible in the rear of his car, stroked the throttle, warming his engine: *Rumppp! Rumppp!* As he did so, the entire front end of the car shook from the power being generated beneath the hood. Snake watched the temperature and oil pressure gauges to make certain no problems were developing. Weasel also now was running toward the line. So were McCulloch's crewmen. At most tracks the cars fire their engines only a short distance from the starting area, but at Indianapolis, the crews had to sprint nearly 150 yards to get to the line. For a moment it looked more like a track meet than a drag race; then the two drivers put their cars in gear and effortlessly drove past their straining crew members to beat them to the bleach box.

Weasel, who already had reached the starting area, guided Snake into the bleach box, then held up both hands as a signal to stop. The bleach box was an area about thirty yards short of the starting line where drivers began their burnouts. There is no box, only an area on the track marked with rubber cones. There is no longer any bleach either, that name meaning the sticky liquid resin that crewmen used to throw under the tires for burnouts. But resin hurts the track surface, and at Indianapolis, crews were required to use plain water from barrels provided or risk disqualification.

Jerry reached into the barrel for a pitcher of water and threw half of it down in front of the left wheel, then ran behind the car to do the same before the right wheel. As he did this, McCulloch was doing his burnout, spinning his tires, warming them, the heat from the tires spinning against pavement, causing large clouds of smoke, actually steam, to rise high in the air. As the heat dried the tires and they grabbed at the pavement, McCulloch shot across the line, darting nearly 100 years up the track. Jerry motioned Snake forward so his rear wheels sat in the water puddles, then pointed down the track, indicating he could go. Jerry was thinking: *Run, car. Just run.*

Weasel had moved off the track to the side, out of Snake's way. There is such an air of frenzy—everybody running, jumping around, noise, cars darting—at the starting line that it is a wonder that more crewmen don't get run down. Don Prudhomme is more careful than most drivers in making sure his crew is clear before he pushes the throttle for a burnout. "He's only hit me twice so far this year," says Jerry. The moment when all thirty-three cars get the green flag and head into the first turn of the Indy 500 is probably the most intense and exciting moment in any sport, but drag racing has its series of mini-dramas each time a pair of race cars, particularly funny cars, come to the line. Some drivers also add an element of show business. Jungle Jim Liberman uses as his chief crewman and bleach pourer his well-built wife who comes to the line dressed in shorts and a skimpy halter. But Liberman had lost in the second round, and there was nothing to distract the spectators from the simple drama of man against man or man against machine.

Snake did his burnout, raising more billowing clouds, and shot across the line to a point near where McCulloch had stopped. The sound was intense, like an explosion that didn't know when to stop. Unless you have stood near a funny car and failed to cover your ears when its driver hit the throttle, you don't know the meaning of noise. It is painful, as though someone were jabbing needles into your ears. The ground shakes. The exhaust from the headers hits you like a hot, evil wind. The driver is protected from most of this because he is inside the car wearing helmet and mask. Those moving near the car have little protection. Weasel wears earplugs similar to those used by target shooters. Jerry wears none. "I kind of like to hear the car," he claims. "I dig cars. I especially dig this car. It turns me on. There's something about a fuel motor that really sounds neat." But after races he gets headaches.

At the moment Snake did his burnout, however, Jerry wasn't thinking about how loud or how neat the engine sounded. Head forward, eyes down, he was moving in the track of the car. "Someday Snake's going to stop," says Jerry, "and I'm going to run right up over his roof."

Jerry was watching the ground so that he could see the exact path that Snake took. Snake had selected a path just to the left of the center of his lane. When Jerry reached the starting line, he stopped, knelt, took a piece of chalk from his pocket, and marked an *X* on the ground exactly where Snake's right rear wheel had passed. At the Nationals, cars are permitted only a single burnout across the line. But at other tracks where second burnouts are permitted, Jerry would have marked the second tire track in chalk with an *O*.

He does this so that when it comes time to stage, Weasel and he can guide Snake directly onto the path of hot rubber that he had just laid down. Rubber already on the track aids traction. But hot rubber provides better traction, especially if the hot rubber on the track is the same compound as the hot rubber on the tires.

Up the track Snake had stopped. Weasel ran forward to guide him back to the line. Strapped into his seat, a funny car driver has no backward vision and has to trust the signals of his crewmen as he backs up. "They're actually the ones driving the car," says Prudhomme, who shoved his gearshift lever into reverse and moved quickly backward. Jerry helped direct Weasel, and Weasel directed Snake. McCulloch had already returned.

Snake signaled Jerry that he wanted more water under his tires to clean them. Jerry reached into the barrel for another bucket and splashed more water under the wheels. *Brrrrt!* Snake revved his engine another time, moving up a few more feet. Then Jerry, who had moved forward with his driver, realized he was standing at the starting line with a pitcher still half full of water and nowhere to throw it. He didn't have time to return to the barrel. He could hardly dump the water in McCulloch's lane. He stood there for a second, momentarily confused, when suddenly a hand reached out and took the pitcher from him. It was starter Buster Couch, who had seen Jerry's plight and knew what to do.

Snake hit his throttle again: *Rummp!* He moved a few feet closer to the line. Once more: *Rummmp!* The car lunged forward. He had tested the clutch now, and he knew the car would hook up to the track. He moved forward slowly. Weasel, using hand signals, guided him into position with his right wheel pointed directly at the *X* that Jerry had chalked on the track. If Snake had come up to the line off the mark, Weasel would have backed him up and made him start all over. If not, he would have heard about it later. The first amber light glowed on the Christmas tree, indicating that Snake's car had moved to within eight inches of the line. Weasel ran to get out of the way.

Jerry already was standing to the side off the track on a patch of grass. Someone came up behind him and asked, "Is this where you stand?" Jerry didn't answer. He was unmoving, frozen in place. He wasn't even blinking his eyelids for fear of missing something. He was staring at the car he loved moving inch by inch up to the line in the most important race of the year and thinking: *Wow! Here we go. This is the last round.*

Ed McCulloch and his crew, meanwhile, had been going through the same process. "The car started," McCulloch later recalled. "We did our smoky burnouts. You let heat build. The hotter the motor gets, to a degree, the more horsepower it will make. I did a short drive. The thing hit hard. It felt good. I backed up again, did a couple of quick moves. Hit it pretty good going to the starting line. It held. The motor sounded good. I felt that I was ready."

Snake moved the front wheel of his car into the second beam. The second amber light flashed in his lane. McCulloch already had put on his second light. The cars were staged.

Prudhomme had been thinking about his rival. "I could see him on the track when he did his burnout. *BRRRRRRRUPPPPPPP!* I saw him take off down the track. I checked him over. Like, I'm out there, and the smoke is clearing out of the cockpit of the car, and before you can start backing up, you look across the track. You kind of look at his pipes. At least I do. I want to see how his car's running. It might be smoking out of one of the pipes. Sometimes I'll back up far enough so I can keep the other driver in sight before I go to the starting line. If he's injured, I want to know about that so when I stage, I don't try to leave real quick and chance red-lighting. It would be horrible to red-light on the last run and have the other car break. He would be able to just putt on down and win," he said.

Buster Couch pressed the button on the box he held in his hand that began the automatic process that would flash first another amber light and, a fifth of a second later, a green.

McCulloch was also aware of the person he was going to race. He commented afterward: "Before I even left, I sat there and looked at him. Looked him over. And he was ready. He had done a couple of blurps to the line and, I mean, she was going to be a good race. Don Prudhomme is a very hard racer. A very, very hard racer."

The amber light near the bottom of the Christmas tree flashed in both lanes. The sound of engines idling on the line already had begun to rise in pitch.

"I saw that he was plenty healthy out there," Don Prudhomme remarked when asked later what he had seen. "Yeah, McCulloch was ready. His car looked as good as it could look. And I figured, he was going to get out on me. And the reason he was going to get out on me was because that's the way my car was set up. Set up so it will run better in the middle of the course. I had to leave the best I could on the starting line, but not let up because at the end I could get him.

"Or at least that's what I thought."

The green lights flashed.

12

"SIX SECONDS"

McCulloch moved first. He reacted the moment he saw amber. A driver who waits until he sees green before he thinks about moving is going to be beaten. Only one-fifth of a second separates the amber and green lights, and in that fifth of a second the brain of the driver first must send a message that says: Move. That message must travel the length of the spinal cord and through the nerves of the right leg to the muscles of the foot. The muscles of the foot must contract and push down on the throttle pedal, which controls the flow of fuel to the engine. The fuel flows. The spark plugs ignite the fuel. The engine, which had been idling at 1,500 rpm, starts to wind. There is an explosion of sound as the revolutions double, and then triple, in a fraction of a second.

At the same moment, a second message is being relayed from the brain to the muscles of the right arm telling it to pull the lever releasing the brake. Prudhomme uses his left hand to hold the steering wheel. Although some drivers release the brake and immediately put a second hand on the steering wheel, Snake likes to drive the entire quarter mile using only the left hand.

His left foot is idle. He braces it against one of the struts inside the car. He uses the left foot only to work the clutch, when they start the engine and when he has to move in reverse. But by the time he has progressed to the starting line, the clutch has already been engaged, and his left foot has no more work to do. The clutch in a funny car is a centrifugal clutch, one that works on engine revolutions, not on springs. As the engine revolutions come up, the clutch snaps shut and launches the car.

A funny car loaded with fuel sitting on the starting line weighs about 2,200 pounds. Moving 2,200 pounds from a dead stop, using tires 112 inches around and 16 inches wide, places great strain on the rear end, the transmission, the crankshaft, right through the valves and rockers of the engine. The many connected parts of the mighty car will literally bend from the strain—and in many cases will *break* before the rubber of the rear tires resting on the track moves the first fraction of an inch. And no matter how well the car, its engine, and its parts are balanced, that rubber will still slip somewhat before the beast moves forward, breaking the beam of light that starts the timing clocks.

So a driver who waits until he sees green before he thinks about moving is going to be beaten.

Both drivers reacted well to the starting lights, McCulloch perhaps a fraction better than Snake. Their official elapsed time would reflect that. But McCulloch had *nailed* his car on the line, slightly depressing the throttle and raising the engine rpms just before launch, so he would have immediate power. Prudhomme, as per plan, had *driven* his car off the line, allowing the engine to remain at idle before going to full power. But there was another factor that permitted McCulloch to move from the line quicker than Snake.

It was a matter of balance. Anybody who has ever ridden a lightweight motorcycle knows that when you apply full power to the rear wheel, that wheel moves forward with such force that it has a tendency to drive right under the front wheel. The result is a wheelstand. Or a *wheelie*. The front wheel bounces up in the air, and the rider has either to lean forward or release power to get the wheel back on the ground.

Racing cars also do wheelies. Some performers at drag meets specialize in driving with their bodies lifted at thirty-degree angles for the entire length of the racetrack. Other racers do wheelies by accident, their front ends flipping so high as they move off the line that they lose the race.

A funny car also will stand on its rear wheels unless it is properly balanced. Although Prudhomme's engine was only sixty inches back of the edge of his front wheel, he had added seventy pounds of weight to hold the front down. McCulloch, however, had balanced his car differently.

Thus, as the light flashed green, his wheels had lifted—just slightly—off the pavement. Unless you were looking for it and knew what to look for, you might not know they had lifted. "My car had been carrying the front end all day," he later explained. "I was doing that for a reason. If the car has the front wheels in the air, it has 100 percent traction on the rear wheels. You can get no more weight transfer." McCulloch could have put more lead on the front axle to keep the front wheels planted on the ground, but he wanted 2,200 pounds pressing down on the rear wheels, holding *them* to the ground. "It launches me harder," was the reason.

When Snake left the line, only his left front wheel raised off the pavement. The reason that the left wheel lifted and not the right is engine torque. The parts of the engine spin clockwise, or from left to right. Thus, this rotary power, or torque, causes more force to be exerted on the right side of the car than on the left. So Snake's right front wheel stayed down. This meant that part of the weight of the car was being carried on it. He had less weight on his rear wheels than his rival, McCulloch, did. Weight over the rear wheels allows those wheels to grip the track better. This was one of the reasons why McCulloch moved off the line better than Snake.

Still another factor was that Snake had removed some of the power from his engine between the semifinals and final runs. He did this by enriching the fuel mixture, and the reason he did it was to avoid smoking the tires as he had against Goldstein. In contrast, McCulloch had added power to his engine by leaning it out. There was no way to take a dynamometer reading of the two engines as they propelled the two cars across the line, so McCulloch's engine may or may not have been stronger at this point. Nevertheless, he moved first.

A hundred feet down the track McCulloch had already taken a good lead on Prudhomme. Jerry and Weasel were standing off to the right as the two cars flew off the starting line, and Jerry believed McCulloch had jumped to almost a full car-length lead. *Oh, boy*, Jerry thought. *Here we go.*

McCulloch's instant lead also bothered Weasel. "We knew Snake planned to drive the car out rather than nail it," he recalled. "But I was nervous. I knew our car runs well down at mid-track. I knew if Snake could stay near him, we could win. But from too far behind, it's hard." Photos of the race, however, later would show that McCulloch did not have as much of a lead as the two crewmen thought. But it still was a lead.

By the time Snake had gone a hundred feet down the track, he could see McCulloch's right front fender. Whenever you can see the other car in a drag race, you're in trouble, because he's probably ahead of you. *Oh, my God*, thought Snake. *No way. He's got me by half a car.*

But even before the two cars reached that point in the race, something occurred that would affect McCulloch's ability to maintain his lead. His car had begun to drift to the right.

McCulloch's car was drifting to the right, and with both front wheels off the ground, he had no way to steer it. It could have been drifting to the right for a number of reasons. The traction of the track under his left wheel might have been slightly better than under his right, causing the left wheel to grip better and pull harder, thus tilting the nose of the car off to the right.

Or the air pressure in the two rear tires may have been slightly different. The air pressure in the rear tires of drag racers is kept very low, only three or four pounds pressure compared to twenty-eight pounds pressure for a normal automobile tire. The rear tires (or slicks, as they're called because of their smooth trackless surface) actually sag and wrinkle, so that when the car first leaves the line, the entire sixteen-inch width of the tire is on the track. As the wheels spin faster, centrifugal force and heat cause the tire to expand, so that crossing the finish line only four to six inches of that surface is on the ground. While they were waiting in the staging area, McCulloch's car had been parked so that the sun was beating down on its right side. This extra heat could have raised the air pressure in that tire ever so slightly, so that the right wheel was putting more rubber down on the pavement than the left.

Or it could have been torque. The same engine force that caused Prudhomme's left wheel to rise, and not his right, may have slightly tilted the body of McCulloch's car, having the same effect as if you tilted an airplane wing.

Or it could have been the breeze that was blowing from the southwest, from the left to the right across the track.

For whichever one of these reasons, or other reasons, or combinations of reasons, McCulloch's car began to drift right toward the center line.

By the time his car had gone fifty feet, he realized that if the drift continued, it would pull him across the center line and cause his disqualification. By the time his car had gone 100 feet, he had reacted to the drift and corrected it. All this took less time to happen that it takes to read this paragraph. Much less time, because it takes a funny car less than one second to move the first 100 feet.

At the same time McCulloch was drifting to the right, Prudhomme was drifting to the left. The two racers, in fact, were on a collision course that, if continued, would cause a devastating crash with neither finalist reaching the finish line. In Prudhomme's case the drift left was for the same reason that had almost caused his disqualification in the second round against Tharp: vibration. Snake recalled and explained later that his car had shaken with vibration in each of the four rounds. He could not explain why, whether it was the track, the tires, or some other factor. But in the final round the vibration was not as severe as it had been in round two, and Snake used his steering wheel to correct, forcing his car back toward the center of the track.

McCulloch cured his drift right by raising his foot ever so slightly from the throttle pedal, feathering it. This lessened ever so little the flow of fuel into the engine. This slowed the acceleration of the car ever so slowly, but was enough to cause the front wheels to slap back down on the ground and enable McCulloch to steer back toward the center of his lane. "I had to lift," he later explained. "I didn't have to get clear out of the throttle, but just enough so the front end could come back down and let me straighten it out. Then I got back on the throttle." McCulloch still had his half-car lead on Don Prudhomme, but he no longer was moving away from him.

The two cars, nearly side by side, screamed off down the track. At the point where McCulloch had feathered his throttle, his engine and that of Snake's already had gone from their 1,500 rpm idling speed to around 7,500 rpm. In the additional 1,200 feet they would travel down the drag strip, the engines would increase only 1,000 rpm's more.

Nevertheless, the cars moved faster and faster. Earlier that year McCulloch had run 4.28 seconds on an eighth-mile track. At Indianapolis' quarter-mile track, he had been clocking about 6.40 seconds. So it would take the two cars more than four seconds to drive the first half of their race and only two seconds to go the second half. And at half track McCulloch still had his half-car lead. He couldn't see Snake's car, but Snake was seeing him all the way. "Six seconds sometimes feels like a lifetime," Don Prudhomme had said, "especially when you look out the side and there's a car right next to you."

"A lot of thoughts go through your mind," McCulloch comments. "What takes six seconds to happen, we could almost write a book about it."

But if McCulloch had lost time correcting for his drift to the right, now Prudhomme would make an error at the point where he should have been catching and passing his rival. He overrevved the engine before shifting from first to second.

Funny cars have two-speed transmissions. They leave the line in first gear, letting the engine revolutions build up, and then shift into the second and higher gear. "You shift by the feel of the car," Snake explained later. "When the car acts like it wants to slow down, you shift. You shift very fast. Just *bam!* You don't lift off the throttle or push in the clutch or anything. Just pull that lever and you fly into another gear."

There is no one best point to pull (or in the case of Mc-Culloch, who had a foot shifter, kick) the lever. Some tracks have several hundred feet of good asphalt near the starting line before they change to a different compound, and drag racers will often shift before they leave the good surface. The same is true if they know they will hit an oily area downtrack. Or if the tires begin to shake, the driver may shift early to try and get rid of the tire shake. "If the car is pulling hard, you run it out," says McCulloch. "I usually shift at about half track. For that round I probably stretched it out pretty good."

McCulloch shifted. And as he did, he thought: *I've got the race won.*

Snake continued even farther down the track. "I just kept winding it in low until the thing almost slowed up. Then I shifted it."

By that time they had gone three-quarters of the way to the finish line with McCulloch maintaining the half-car lead he had gained at the start. They had barely a second remaining in the race. Like this much: *One-hundred-one.* Say it, and the race would be over.

McCulloch, Snake thought. *You are either history or the winner.*

Back at the starting line, Weasel and Jerry, neither one of them having moved an inch in the six seconds, fixed their eyes on the two cars moving away from them. *Move, car,* thought Jerry. *Make your move!*

And Snake's car began to move. He began to close the gap.

As McCulloch approached the first timing light, only sixty-six feet from the finish line, he glanced to his right, and didn't see the other driver. But as they crossed the finish line, he saw a flash of yellow at his side. Out of the corner of his eye he saw it: a flash of yellow. Like, *flick!* It was there. By the time they had reached the second timing light, sixty-six feet beyond the finish line, he saw that Prudhomme was in front of him. But at what point had he passed?

"I didn't know who won," McCulloch later recalled. "It was that close. But I thought maybe I did get there first."

"I knew it was close in the lights," Prudhomme later recalled. "But I thought maybe I had beat him."

As was his custom, Don Prudhomme continued straight down the track, taking the entire length of it to slow his racer, his blue parachute twisting behind him as he went all the way to the pavement's end.

Ed McCulloch, meanwhile, braked earlier and turned off at the first exit road. It was at that moment he got his first clue to who had been victorious. He glanced out his side window at the cameramen for ABC television, who were filming the event for *Wide World of Sports*. They were turning away from him and starting up the track to go interview Don Prudhomme.

Epilogue

"AND IT WAS SO-O-O CLOSE"

Several months after Don Prudhomme's victory at the Nationals, I sat in his living room to watch a videotape of the *Wide World of Sports* telecast of the event. Jerry and Weasel had dropped by. His wife, Lynn, also watched. "Now we have the funny cars," the voice of announcer Keith Jackson echoed from the TV set. "These are the wild ones. And it's Don Prudhomme of Granada Hills, California. He has won the top fuel championship here at the Nationals three times. He's going for his first funny car championship, and he'll be racing Richard Tharp out of Dallas, Texas."

Snake sat at one end of the living room, his hands folded over his chest, his feet up on the coffee table, seeming to betray no emotion as he watched. "Tharp wasn't running that good," he admitted in a soft voice, "and I really messed up because I cooled it on the starting line. I didn't get into it hard enough."

On the screen the two cars rushed off the line with Tharp momentarily in the lead. Then Snake's yellow Cuda began to move. "And it's Prudhomme at the top end!" shouted Jackson.

Snake looked toward me and laughed. "Boy, that car runs good!"

Now the question," Jackson continued, as the screen showed a slow-motion shot of Snake veering toward the center line. "Did he cross that dividing line? You can touch it, but you can't cross it. Did he cross it?"

"Nahhh," said Don Prudhomme.

The telecast showed a second, then a third replay of that moment, including one from a camera positioned near the start. "Here's the shot we saw," said Jerry. "I thought Buster was going to punch me that one time. I bumped the starting light, and he got hot."

"Buster's the NHRA starter," explained Don. "He likes to run the show, and he likes to exhibit his authority now and then. He likes to say, 'You're out,' and that's it."

"He don't like to hear nothing from nobody," said Weasel.

"Yeah," said Snake, "whereas I want to fight about it a little bit. I just don't go out that easy."

The scene on the screen shifted to Ed McCulloch's quarterfinal run against Bobby Rowe followed by an interview where Keith Jackson asked McCulloch about tire vibration. "Well, I believe the tires are gripping too much," McCulloch responded. "There are two ways to cure it: You have to pull more clutch out of it, let the clutch slip more, or build more horsepower to get up on the tires so it will not shake."

Watching this, Don Prudhomme said very quietly, "We know something he doesn't know."

After Snake's semifinal victory over Goldstein, there was another slow-motion shot. "You're going to see that Don Prudhomme popped his chute before he went into that speed trap," Keith Jackson instructed the television audience. I asked Snake for his comment.

"Well, I have a habit of doing that," he confessed. "But let's face it: it's not the first time I've driven the car. It's like free-falling from an airplane. If you pull the ripcord often enough, you know just about where it's going to catch. And the main reason I do that is we've run on so many of these grim tracks where if you run that thing all the way through and don't hit the chute until the last light, you're in serious trouble. So I go for the chute going into the lights. I go: *'Ehhhhh—Now!'* I haven't gotten beat doing it yet."

Then there was the inevitable replay of the finals of the 1970 Nationals, the time when Jim Nicoll's car exploded at the finish line, the shot of Prudhomme, at a moment when he thought Nicoll dead, saying he was going to quit. Snake watched the scenes unemotionally, then growled, "That no-good Nicoll beat us last weekend."

Finally came the race between McCulloch and Prudhomme, a freeze frame of their two cars crossing the line. Prudhomme had run 6.38, going 229.59 mph. McCulloch had run 6.44, going 226.70 mph. "And it was so-o-o-o close," drawled the voice of Keith Jackson. At the far end of the track, Jackson had stuck a microphone under Don Prudhomme's chin. "Hey, Don. Congratulations."

"Thank you."

"You won three top fuel titles, and now a funny car. Four national titles at Indianapolis."

"Yeah, I guess so. We're really happy. This is the first time we won the National event in our funny car. As I was telling you earlier today. And we also ran in the 6:20s with it, and we just, uh—I was very happy. I don't know what to say. Thanks to Goodyear and all my sponsors: Wynn's Oil, Coke."

"Great week for you."

"Thank you very much."

Then the picture on the screen faded. In his living room Don Prudhomme turned to his two crewmen, who had been caught by the TV cameras in a moment of wild, uncontrollable joy, jumping up and down at the starting line, pounding each other deliriously. "You guys are going to cool it today, huh?"

Later, when we were alone, I talked some more with Snake about his victories that one day in September at Indianapolis over Prock, Tharp, Goldstein, and McCulloch. "When you look back at those four runs, think of how easy it would have been for you to miss the top prize," I suggested. "In the first round Prock ran the third fastest e.t. of the meet behind you. If your car had run just a shade slower, you would have been history."

"Sure," Snake admitted.

"In the second round, you almost got disqualified."

"Right."

"And the third round, you smoked your tires and ran poorly. The only thing that saved you is that Goldstein smoked his tires, too, and ran even worse."

"That's absolutely correct."

"Then you and McCulloch ran a near dead heat. So forget that you were the fastest qualifier, that you set a national e.t. record, that you completely dominated the meet by your presence; only a thread separated you from fame and obscurity."

"No question about it," Snake agreed. "No matter how well you run the round before, when you come up to the line again, it's like a whole new event. It's almost like going to a different day. Anything can happen. The other guy you're racing isn't beat no matter how slow he's been running. You go up to the starting line thinking the money is in the bank, but you can't collect it until after the light comes on at the end."

Stacked side by side on a closet shelf in the guest bedroom of his Granada Hills home are the four trophies Don Prudhomme has won at the Nationals.* Nobody has more. Yet in 1965 he had hidden behind a tree before the finals, hoping he wouldn't have to run. In 1969 a sudden rain shower gave him time to change a broken engine. In 1970 he barely edged Nicoll at the finish line. In 1973 the same was true in his race with McCulloch. Had the circumstances in each of these four instances been slightly different, Don Prudhomme's shelf would have been bare. Yet he is the dominant figure in drag racing today—and probably will be for years to come. I asked Snake what lay in his future.

*Don Prudhomme added a fifth trophy to this collection in 1974, winning the funny car title at Indy again.

He responded only after some thought: "I don't feel I've accomplished enough. Someday I really want to be ahead of the pack. I want to win even more. I guess Don Garlits is one of the guys who really keeps me going, because I want to someday win more events than he has won and surpass what he's done, and that's going to be a tough job."

I suggested that he already had won one more title at the Nationals than Garlits.

"Yeah," Snake admitted, "but there are still challenges. Think of Garlits today: forty-two years old going up and down that track. I used to say to myself: I don't want to be doing that when I'm forty-two. But the more I think about it, I probably will. Because it's gotten to be a kind of thing with me. If he's that good at forty-two, I'll be better. I'm ten years younger. See, by the time I'm forty-two I'll win a lot more championships than he ever thought of winning. You know what I mean? And I've told him that: 'Think of all the races I'll have won by the time I'm your age.' He doesn't like that."

Don Prudhomme is respected by other racers, even admired, but not always liked. He knows his ability and makes little effort to conceal it. "I admit I'm cocky," he says. In addition, he has a ferocious temper, which he vents when provoked. Engine builder Ed Pink admits that he is careful which of his men he assigns to Snake because Snake can be very demanding and difficult to work with. Yet he can also be gentle, thoughtful, relaxed, friendly, and can have of a good sense of humor. He is more likely to display these attributes away from a racetrack than at one.

Among the many photographs of Don Prudhomme I took at Indianapolis and at other racetracks while researching this book, I have one favorite. It is not the best photograph, but it comes closest to portraying what makes him a winner. I took the picture before I got to know Snake well, before I had stayed at his house. It was on one of the practice days for the Nationals, and Snake was moving his car up to the line for a qualification run. I focused on him as he was walking toward the staging lanes, arms on his hips, an expression on his face that was half smile, half scowl. I snapped the picture just as he glanced up and saw me. Anybody who knows Snake can tell exactly what is going through his mind. He was thinking: *Get out of my way!*

"Sometimes I think I've done it all," Snake said in summing up his career, "but I really haven't." He paused. Through the glass doors of his living room, he could see out across the valley. He could see ahead to a lot of six-second runs. And five-second runs. And maybe even someday, four-second runs. "It goes on and on," said Don Prudhomme.

About the Author

Hal Higdon is the author of thirty-four books, including the best-selling title, *Marathon: The Ultimate Training Guide*. He is also a longtime contributor to *Runner's World* magazine. He ran eight times in the Olympic Trials and won four World Masters Championships. One of the founders of the Road Runners Club of America (RRCA), he serves as a training consultant for many races and provides interactive training programs and online guidance.

In addition to his popular works on sports and running, Higdon is the author of *The Horse That Played Center Field*, a children's book that was made into an animated feature by ABC-TV. He was also a finalist in NASA's Journalist-in-Space program. In 2003, the American Society of Journalists and Authors awarded Higdon with its Career Achievement Award, the highest honor given to writer members. Hal Higdon lives in Long Beach, Indiana, with his wife, Rose. They have three adult children and nine grandchildren.

Index